A Contemporary Perspective on
LMS Railway Signalling
VOL 2

A Contemporary Perspective on
LMS Railway Signalling
VOL 2
Semaphore Swansong

Allen Jackson

THE CROWOOD PRESS

First published in 2015 by
The Crowood Press Ltd
Ramsbury, Marlborough
Wiltshire SN8 2HR

www.crowood.com

British Library Cataloguing-in-Publication Data
A catalogue record for this book is available from the British Library.

ISBN 978 1 78500 072 0

Dedication
For Ninette.

Acknowledgements
The kindness and interest shown by railway signallers,
including David Dawson, David Horton, Alan Roberts.

Frontispiece: Llandudno station signals and box, January 2015.

Typeset by Bookcraft Ltd, Stroud, Gloucestershire
Printed and bound in Malaysia by Times Offset (M) Sdn Bhd

Contents

Preface

The GWR book in this series concentrated more on the ways of working, and while it would be easy and more lucrative to refer readers back to that volume, some explanations of those features have been incorporated in this work. I apologize if this seems slightly repetitive if you have already read the GWR book but I feel there will be some who have not. In addition the Scottish ways of working differ somewhat, so they are explained here.

Many main lines have not seen mechanical signalling for thirty or more years, and so the emphasis tends to be on the secondary lines.

The survey of what is left of the mechanical signalling on Network Rail took place from 2003 and 2015, really at the advent of usable digital photography.

While this was being done some of it disappeared before I could get to it and so there may be omissions.

With improvements in digital equipment and the means to pay for it, a good deal of what remains has been revisited in the last twelve months.

Fig. 1   Stirling Middle signal box with some of its signals, August 2003.

Introduction

Up until 1 January 1923 there were hundreds of railway companies in Britain. The government at the time perceived an administrative difficulty in controlling the railways' activities at times of national crisis. The country had just endured World War I and the feeling was that it could all be managed better if they were amalgamated. Thus came the railway 'grouping' as it was termed, creating just four railway companies.

The London Midland and Scottish Railway was one of those four entities but the identities of the larger companies within it persisted and does so to this day. Lines are referred to by their pre-grouping ownership even now. This is often because routes were duplicated and so it was never going to be accurate to refer to the line from 'London to Birmingham' without the qualification 'London and North Western', if that was the one being referred to. This was to differentiate it from the lines run by the Great Western.

Many of the smaller companies did lose their identity, in signalling terms, although their architecture may remain.

The only pre-grouping railways considered therefore are those for which an identifiable signalling presence existed at the time of the survey.

There are so many ex-LMS signal boxes and infrastructure that it has been necessary to split the LMS into two.

Volume 1 covers:

- Midland Railway (MR)
- Lancashire and Yorkshire Railway (L&YR)
- Furness Railway (FR)
- Glasgow and South Western Railway (GSWR)
- North Staffordshire Railway (NSR)

Volume 2 covers:

- London and North Western Railway (LNWR)
- Caledonian Railway (CR)
- Highland Railway (HR)

This splits the journeys to the North and Scotland into two distinct routes: Volume 1 covers the Midland over the Settle–Carlisle, then GSWR to Glasgow; while Volume 2 covers the LNWR and CR route of the West Coast Main Line and on by the Highland Railway to Inverness.

In the book the system of units used is the imperial system which is what the railways themselves still use, although there has been a move to introduce metric units in places like the Railway Accident Investigation Branch reports and in the south-east of England where there are connections to the Channel Tunnel.

- 1 mile = 1.6km
- 1 yard = 0.92m
- 1 chain = 20.11m
- 1 chain = 22yd
- 1 mile = 1,760yd or 80 chains

CHAPTER I

Signal Boxes and Infrastructure on Network Rail

The survey was carried out between 2003 and 2015 and represents a wide cross-section of the remaining signal boxes on Network Rail. Inevitably some have closed and been demolished, while others have been preserved and moved away since the survey started. The large numbers of retired or preserved signalling structures have not been considered in this work and are to be held over for a future volume.

Although the book is organized around the pre-grouping companies, the passage of time has meant that some pre-grouping structures have been replaced by LMS or BR buildings.

If you are intending visiting any of them it is suggested that you find out what the current status is before you set off.

For reasons of access and position some signal boxes are covered in greater detail than others and some are featured as a 'focus on', where the quality of the information or the interest of that location merits that attention.

Some of the signal boxes have been reduced in status over the years, and while they may have controlled block sections or main lines in the past, some no longer do so but are (or were at the time of the survey) on Network Rail's payroll as working signal boxes.

Details of the numbers of levers are included but not all the levers may be fully functional, as signal boxes have been constantly modified over the years.

Lever colours are:

Red	Home signals
Yellow	Distant signals
Black	Points
Blue	Facing point locks
Blue/brown	Wicket gates at level crossings
Black/Yellow chevrons	Detonator placers
White	Not in use
Green	King lever to cancel locking when box switched out

Levers under the block shelf or towards the front window normally are said to be normal, and those pulled over to the rear of the box are said to be reversed.

There are some boxes where the levers are mounted the opposite way round, in other words levers in the normal position point to the rear wall, but the convention remains the same.

Listed Buildings

Many signal boxes are considered to have architectural or historic merit and are Grade II listed by English Heritage or Historic Scotland. This basically means they cannot be changed externally without permission. If the owner allows the building to decay to such an extent that it is unsafe, the building can then be demolished. The number of signal boxes with a listing is due to increase on the news that they are all to be replaced by 2020.

A Grade I listing would require the interiors to remain the same so that is unlikely to happen with Network Rail structures but may happen with the preservation movement – many boxes have had the interiors preserved as fully operational working museums.

In Scotland the classification system is somewhat different and is as follows: Category A for buildings of national or international architectural worth or intrinsic merit; Category B for buildings of regional architectural worth or intrinsic merit; Category C for buildings of local importance, architectural worth or intrinsic merit.

Signal Box Official Abbreviations

Most signal boxes on Network Rail have an official abbreviation of one, two or sometimes three letters. This usually appears on all signal posts relevant to that box. Finding an abbreviation could be tricky – for example there are eight signal boxes with Norton in the title – until you realize that they are not unique. The abbreviation for each box appears after the box title in this book, if it has one.

Ways of Working

Absolute Block – AB

A concept used almost since railways began is the 'block' of track where a train is permitted to move from block to block provided no other train is in the block being moved to. This relies on there being up and down tracks. Single lines have their own arrangements. It is usual to consider trains travelling towards London to be heading in the up direction, but there are local variations and this is made clear in the text.

This block system was worked by block instruments that conveyed the track occupancy status and by a bell system that was used to communicate with adjacent signal boxes.

Signal Box A		Signal Box B	
Activity	Bell Code	Activity	Bell Code
Call attention	I	Acknowledge	I
Line clear for express?	4	Acknowledge Line is clear for express	4
Train entering block section	2	Acknowledge Train entering block section	2
Acknowledge Train leaving block section	2.I	**Train leaving block section**	2.I

The signallers rely on single-stroke bells for box-to-box communication – although this is supplemented by more modern means, the passage of trains is still controlled this way. A typical communication for the passage of an express passenger train (Network Rail Class 1) from signal box A to signal box B would be as shown on page 9; the text in **bold** is the instigator and that in plain text the reply.

Each time an action is carried out, the train's situation is recorded on Signal Box A's instrument and reflected by block instruments by the signaller at Signal Box B, who is the receiving box.

The status of a block can be one of the following:

Normal – Line Blocked
Line Clear
Train on Line

This procedure is repeated along the line to subsequent signal boxes. The absolute block system refers to double lines and the above procedure is designed for one line of track only. With double track it is not unusual to have two sets of dialogue between adjacent boxes as trains pass each other on separate lines.

In our example, although only the up line has been shown, a train could be travelling from A to B on the up line and another train on the down line from B to A.

Track Circuit Block – TCB

Track circuit block is really all to do with colour light signals, which, strictly speaking are outside the scope of this book, except that many signal boxes interface to track circuit block sections and will have track circuit block equipment or indications in them.

Originally track circuits lit a lamp in a signal box to indicate where a train was. Then they were used to interlock block instruments, signals and points together to provide a safe working semaphore signal environment.

With colour light signals it is possible to provide automatically changing signals that are controlled by the passage of trains or presence of vehicles on the track. The Train Out of Section of AB working can be reproduced technologically by using axle counters. To quote the memorable words of BBC reporter Brian Hanrahan during the Falklands War – 'I counted them all out and I counted them all back' – that's all axle counters do and if the numbers are not equal, signals are turned to red.

Single Line Workings

These – key token, tokenless block and no signaller key token, one train working and one train staff – are covered in detail in the section on the signal box that supervises such workings.

The suffix (i) behind a box title indicates interior views.

Fig 2   Class 156, 156 472 approaches Wigton station under the eagle eye of the signaller on the Cumbrian Coast Line, December 2014.

Summary of Disposition LMS Volume 2

London and North Western Railway

Whitehaven to Carlisle
- Bransty
- Parton
- Workington Main No. 2
- Workington Main No. 3
- Maryport
- Wigton

North Lancashire
- Bare Lane
- Hest Bank Level Crossing Frame

Crewe to Shrewsbury
- Gresty Lane No. 1
- Nantwich
- Wrenbury
- Whitchurch
- Prees
- Wem
- Harlescott Crossing
- Crewe Bank
- Crewe Junction
- Severn Bridge Junction

Crewe to Chester and Holyhead
- Crewe Steel Works
- Beeston Castle and Tarporley
- Mold Junction
- Sandycroft
- Rockcliffe Hall
- Holywell Junction
- Mostyn
- Talacre
- Prestatyn (i)
- Rhyl
- Abergele
- Llandudno Junction

Llandudno Branch
- Deganwy
- Llandudno

Blaenau Ffestiniog Branch
- Glan Conway Station

- Llanrwst North
- Blaenau Ffestiniog Station
- Penmaenmawr
- Bangor
- Llanfair Level Crossing
- Gaerwen
- Tŷ Croes
- Valley
- Holyhead

Manchester to Buxton
- Hazel Grove
- Norbury Crossing (i)
- Furness Vale
- Chapel-en-le-Frith
- Buxton

Wirral and Runcorn
- Runcorn
- Halton Junction
- Frodsham Junction
- Norton
- Helsby Junction
- Stanlow and Thornton
- Ellesmere Port
- Hooton
- Canning Street North

Widnes to Warrington
- Carterhouse Junction
- Fidlers Ferry
- Monks Siding
- Litton's Mill Crossing
- Crosfields Crossing
- Arpley Junction

Manchester Area
- Diggle Junction
- Denton Junction
- Eccles
- Heaton Norris Junction
- Stockport No. 2
- Stockport No. 1
- Edgeley Junction No. 2
- Edgeley Junction No. 1

Liverpool Area
- Astley
- Rainhill
- Huyton
- Prescot
- St Helens Station
- Edge Hill
- Liverpool Lime Street
- Allerton Junction
- Speke Junction

South Cheshire
- Macclesfield
- Winsford
- Crewe Coal Yard
- Salop Goods Junction
- Crewe Sorting Sidings North
- Basford Hall Junction

Staffordshire
- Stafford No. 5
- Stafford No. 4

The Chase Line
- Brereton Sidings
- Hednesford
- Bloxwich
- Lichfield Trent Valley No. 1
- Lichfield Trent Valley Junction
- Alrewas
- Tamworth Low Level

West Yorkshire
- Batley

South Midlands
- Watery Lane Shunt Frame
- Narborough
- Croft
- Coundon Road Station
- Hawkesbury Lane

Caledonian Railway
Clyde–Forth Valley to Perth
- Carmuirs West Junction
- Larbert Junction
- Larbert North
- Plean Junction
- Stirling Middle
- Stirling North
- Dunblane
- Greenloaning
- Blackford
- Auchterarder
- Hilton Junction
- Fouldubs Junction

Perth to Aberdeen
- Barnhill
- Errol
- Longforgan
- Carnoustie
- Craigo
- Laurencekirk
- Carmont
- Stonehaven
- Newtonhill

Glasgow
- Barrhead

Highland Railway
- Stanley Junction
- Dunkeld
- Pitlochry
- Blair Atholl
- Dalwhinnie
- Kingussie
- Aviemore
- Nairn
- Forres
- Elgin

This does not claim to be an all-encompassing list and there are odd stragglers that were not surveyed and are now no more.

CHAPTER 2

London and North Western Railway (LNWR)

The LNWR was one of the early creations of railway companies from a merger of three: the Grand Junction, London and Birmingham and the Manchester and Birmingham. It styled itself the 'Premier Line' and in the late nineteenth century was the largest joint stock company in the world. From the amalgamation it linked most of the major cities in England west of the Pennines and was the rival to the Great Northern and North Eastern for the railway equivalent of the 'blue riband' of the route to Scotland. It formed what is now the West Coast Main Line (WCML).

The heyday of railways is generally accepted to be before World War I and the LNWR had then a route mileage of 1,500 miles (2,400km) and employed 111,000 people. In addition to the WCML the LNWR was also acknowledged as the main route to Ireland through the port of Holyhead, and the Irish Mail is the oldest named train in the world.

In common with other major routes it has seen much modernization and automation in terms of railway signalling such that at the major centres the mechanical scene is either thin on the ground or non-existent. However, some routes in the northwest of England and North Wales and Scotland had largely escaped the worst of the cull at the time of the survey.

Whitehaven to Carlisle

This section covers the remaining boxes on the former LNWR line around the Cumbrian coast and a couple of boxes in North Lancashire around the Morecambe Bay area that are no longer in service. Fig. 3 depicts a not-to-scale schematic diagram of the area and the connections to other railway companies.

The Cumbrian coast is wild and spectacular with mountains as a backdrop and yet saw intensive coal mining and iron and steel production in the nineteenth century. Many traces of the former industrial past have receded or disappeared leaving a coastline reverting to its largely unspoilt origins.

Bransty (BY)

Date Built	1899
LNWR Type or Builder	LNWR Type 4+
No. of Levers	60
Ways of Working	KT, AB
Current Status	Active
Listed (Y/N)	N

This part of the journey starts at Whitehaven, which is well known as a port and for its rugby

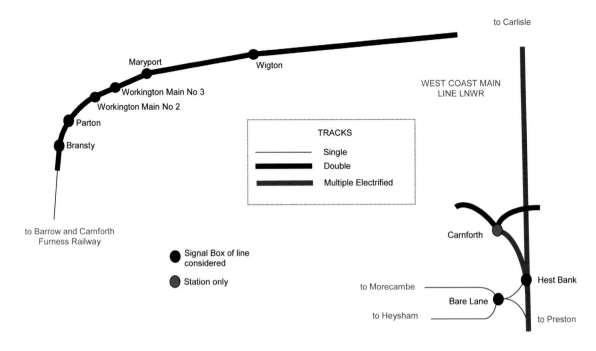

Fig. 3   Cumbria and North Lancashire schematic diagram.

league team. It also was the venue for the last invasion of England by John Paul Jones in 1778 during the American War of Independence.

The town has strong employment links to the Sellafield nuclear plant down the coast in Furness Railway territory.

The box near Whitehaven station is named Bransty and was originally Bransty No. 2 – a change typical of a pared-down railway system that was once much busier. The view in Fig. 4 was taken

in 2006 and was selected as a recent visit in 2014 revealed a complex of Network Rail buildings next to the box, obscuring some of the detail. The box now (2014) controls the signals of the former Parton signal box, our next stop up the line. The section of single line south towards St Bees is worked by key token and the boundary between LNWR and Furness Railways was between Whitehaven and St Bees.

The overview of the layout is shown in Fig. 5 with the sea in attendance behind the station and box. The station looks as though it had three platforms and, by the state of the rear platform face, nearest the camera, four platforms originally. Two now remain, of which platform 1, nearest the Tesco store, is a bay platform for the shuttle service to Carlisle. Platform 2, next up and nearer the camera, is the single line from St Bees coming in from the left

Fig. 4   Bransty signal box, November 2006.

Fig. 5   Overview of Whitehaven
station, November 2006.

and going out towards Carlisle past the box on the right. It becomes double track again shortly thereafter. Platform 3 is still optimistically signed as such as if expecting track to be relaid anytime soon.

In Fig. 6, a class 156 is arriving from Carlisle into platform 2 heading for St Bees and Barrow-in-Furness on the single line, and will require a token to proceed. The view is from the Carlisle bay and up towards the double track to Parton and Carlisle. The two home signals have anti-climb panels fitted to the ladders. The semaphore in the distance is for the down main line to Carlisle, which is on the left.

The 1,283yd (1,173m) Whitehaven tunnel portal in Fig. 7 frames platform 2 at Whitehaven, and an LED colour light signal guards the way to the single track to St Bees and Barrow-in-Furness. The sharp curve on platform 2 needs not only a check rail but a flange greaser to prevent excessive wear.

Key Token

The grey box in front of the signal post is inscribed with the legend 'TOKEN C'BOARD' and houses the auxiliary key token instrument that enables the driver of a train bound for St Bees to help themselves, as it were. As the two token instruments here and at St Bees are electrically interlocked, only one token may be withdrawn at once, meaning only one train can proceed along a single line in the one direction. On some installations it is possible to withdraw a further token from the same instrument for a train travelling in the same direction for which a token has already been issued, but is still

Fig. 6   Class 156 arrives at Whitehaven, December 2014.

Fig. 7   Whitehaven platform 2 with token cupboard, December 2014.

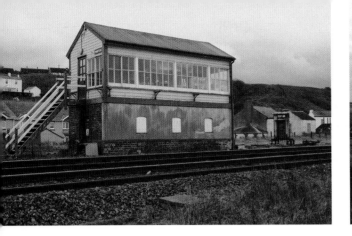

Fig. 8   Parton signal box, November 2006.

Fig. 9   Parton looking towards Carlisle, November 2006.

under full signal control. The token is the driver's authority to proceed, and accidents have happened where a driver has been issued the token for the wrong line by a signaller. This only happened where the journey was single line in both directions. At Whitehaven the line becomes double track towards Carlisle. The token can also literally be the key, known as Annett's key, by which ground frame points can be unlocked whilst in the section.

Bransty signal box is an endpoint for mileage calculations – it is 74 miles 73 chains (120.6km) from Carnforth station junction, while heading northwards towards Parton and Carlisle the count starts at zero.

Fig. 10   Parton looking towards Whitehaven, November 2006.

Parton (PS)

Date Built	1879
LNWR Type or Builder	LNWR Type 4+
No. of Levers	28
Ways of Working	AB
Current Status	Demolished 2010
Listed (Y/N)	N

Parton is a real seaside village, and the station and box were on a sea wall that seems to form part of Parton's defences. Unfortunately the box must have been under severe attack from the weather and had to be demolished in May 2010 due to its poor condition.

In Fig. 8 you can see Parton signal box is really under the cosh, with a concrete wall to protect and

underpin the front of the box. The station platforms are just to the right of the box.

Fig. 9 is the view towards Carlisle from the down platform. The green hut building near the box is a lamp oil store – oddly in 2006 oil lamps were still in use here. Oil lamps have been replaced by electric lamps with either filaments or light-emitting diodes, LEDs. Lamps would need to be taken down once a week and filled with oil and trimmed before being replaced back up the signals posts.

On the same platform as Fig. 9, the view in Fig. 10 is now looking towards Whitehaven and Barrow-in-Furness. The sea and the lighthouse emphasize the proximity of the coast to the station. The railway forms part of the sea defences for this part of the coast and a small tunnel under the railway gives access to a car park and the beach.

Parton signal box was 1 mile and 41 chains (2.4km) from Bransty signal box.

Workington Main No. 2 (WM2)

Date Built	1889
LNWR Type or Builder	LNWR Type 4+
No. of Levers	58
Ways of Working	AB
Current Status	Active
Listed (Y/N)	N

Workington lies at the mouth of one of the Rivers Derwent and there has been habitation there since Roman times.

It may seem a bit off the beaten track for heavy industry but was a centre for coal and the quarrying of high-grade iron ore. Workington, at one point, had the first large-scale steelworks in the country when all the rest were producing just iron in industrial quantities.

The steel plant that developed as a result quickly gained a reputation for high-quality steels, in particular rails for track. With the continued development of continuously welded rail in use in Britain, the plant at Workington was deemed to be not capable of producing rail to the required lengths. This facility was then transferred to Scunthorpe, after some

delay. There is still a steel presence in Workington in the shape of Tata Steel, who manufacture continuous casting machines. The port is still in being and is rail connected and was originally owned by the steel company. Workington did manufacture vehicles at one point and the Pacer class 142 DMUs were made here.

The railway facilities reflected the industrial base – there were several signal boxes as well as a handsome station and steam locomotive engine sheds. The latter existed until recent years when it was dismantled for use by the Great Central preserved railway at Loughborough in Leicestershire.

The first box encountered in Workington, travelling north from Parton, is No. 2. The box, in Fig. 11, is flanked by Workington freight yard just south of the box, and beyond the road overbridge even further south is the remains of the Corus Track Products works. Opposite the box was the steam locomotive depot.

Fig. 12 is looking north towards Workington station, and the former Workington yard is to the left of the main running lines. The yard still has manual point levers and a loading gauge frame on the far left that was used to check the height of loaded wagons to ensure they would fit under bridges and tunnels. The gauge frame is missing the curved metal gauge suspended from the gallows bracket.

The canopies of the station platforms can just be seen at the extreme top right of the picture. The

Fig. 11   Workington Main No. 2 signal box, November 2006.

Fig. 12   Site of former goods yard and engine sheds at Workington, December 2014.

Fig. 13 Workington Main No. 2 signals, December 2014.	Fig. 14 Workington looking towards Whitehaven, December 2014.

entry to the former steam depot is visible to the right of the main running lines.

The view in the opposite direction is shown in Fig. 13. The up main starter colour light signal from the up platform towards Parton is signal WM2 5, and the semaphore is the starter from the reception siding that is connected to the yard behind the box. There is a crossover to enable trains leaving the reception sidings to gain the up main line. The sidings on the near left are first of all a bay platform, nearest the running line, and then carriage sidings, some part of which had been enclosed.

The final view of Workington Main No. 2 and the layout is looking towards Parton and the outer home colour light signal in Fig. 14. The track plant yard is still there on the right. It was closed in August 2006. The overgrown track on the left is the headshunt for the steam locomotive depot and no doubt this would be used to shunt coal wagons to keep the locos supplied.

Workington Main No. 2 signal box is 6 miles 53 chains (10.7km) from Bransty signal box.

Workington Main No. 3 (WM3)

Date Built	1886
LNWR Type or Builder	LNWR Type 4+
No. of Levers	25
Ways of Working	AB
Current Status	Active
Listed (Y/N)	N

Workington Main No. 3 had originally been a fifty-five-lever box when the branch line to Buckhill and Calva Junction had been in operation.

The box is seen in Fig. 15 at the Carlisle end of the up platform at Workington station; the two tracks in the centre are termed the middle sidings, although they were until recently loops. Note that there is still bullhead rail on the sidings.

The signal box controls not only the Carlisle end of the station and its approaches but also the reception siding down exit. The box also releases access to the ground frame for the Workington Docks line.

Fig. 16 shows the Workington Main No. 3 approaches from Carlisle. The subsidiary signal arm on the bracket is for the reception siding for the goods yard, accessed over the crossover. The distant signal is Workington Main No. 2's as the boxes are so close together. A warning, in the shape of the distant signal, as to the status of No. 2's home

Fig. 15 Workington Main No. 3 signal box, November 2006.

Fig. 16   Workington approaches from Carlisle, November 2006.

Fig. 17   Workington station, Carlisle end, November 2006.

signal has to be given at this point to enable a train to be ready to stop if required at No. 2's home signal. This is WM2 5, which we saw earlier. The two rods leading up to the point by the bracket signal contain one for the crossover and one for the facing point locks. The docks branch is on the left-hand side within half a mile of the home signal.

Fig. 17 is looking back the other way towards the box and the station. The box is tucked behind the road overbridge and the middle sidings are also on view, both of which have trap points. The track on the right is the exit from the reception siding, actually a loop, with its starter signal. The trap point has a facing-point lock on it and the reception loop is also track circuited.

Fig. 18 is a view of Workington station and No. 3 box looking towards Carlisle. Worthy of note is

how the platforms are only white-edged for about 80yd on each side, enough for a two-car unit. The canopies have been similarly cut down to fit. On the right is evidence of a train stabling facility with an inspection platform, hosepipes and floodlights. The vertical wooden battens on the end of the station building would have supported advertisement hoardings. The two middle roads would only have contained freight or passenger empty stock trains as their exits are controlled only by ground discs and they are not track circuited. The third ground disc on the right is for a reversing move over the crossover from the up main line on the right.

The two semaphores on the left are the platform starter and, on the extreme left, the reception siding starter; from the white lozenge on the front of each post, these lines are track circuited.

Fig. 18   Workington station,
November 2006.

Fig. 19   Workington station, December 2014.

Fig. 19 is the same view as Fig. 18 but zoomed in a little and eight years later. The box has been plasticized and the middle sidings are now disconnected from the up and down running lines at the No. 3 signal box end. No one told the ground discs, though, and they are still in place. The station buildings remain well kept although the mower could use a workout.

Workington Main No. 3 signal box is 6 miles 74 chains (11.1km) from Bransty signal box.

Maryport (MS)

Date Built	1933
LNWR Type or Builder	LMS Type 11b+
No. of Levers	50
Ways of Working	AB
Current Status	Active
Listed (Y/N)	N

The original line from Carlisle was the Maryport and Carlisle Railway, before it became subsumed into the LMS in 1923. Built in 1836, it was an early and very profitable line constructed to tap the collieries' output near Maryport and bring it to Carlisle for onward shipment. Its location meant that it had a virtual monopoly over the extensive coal traffic and this ensured success.

Fig. 20 is Maryport Station signal box; the signals are plated MS but the box is officially known just as Maryport. The signals and points have been modernized and this is usual where a box has to work facilities that are some distance from it. In this case there is an opencast coal site that has a loop

and siding about a mile (1.5km) from the box in the Workington direction. This would make it impractical to use mechanical equipment here. Rod- and lever-operated points can be a maximum of 450yd (410m) from the box before they need to be power operated.

The layout at Maryport looking towards Workington and the opencast site is shown in Fig. 21. The track consists of a pair of loops that enable freight trains to bypass the single-platform station. The platform has crossovers at each end to enable passenger trains to gain the correct line. A passenger train leaving the platform shown would be signalled by MS 31 to leave via the crossover to go under the bridge on the left-hand side up running line to Workington. The elevated 'ground disc'-replacement LED signal below the main aspect on signal 31 is for the siding whose headshunt buffer stop can be seen past the bridge.

Fig. 22 shows the other direction on the single platform and the crossover access to the running

Fig. 20   Maryport Station signal box, November 2006.

Fig. 21   Maryport looking towards Workington, December 2014.

Fig. 22   Maryport looking towards Carlisle, December 2014.

lines. The incoming colour light signal just after the bridge has a 'feather' on it to signal a move into the platform from Carlisle. Signal MS 45 refers to the down main line towards Carlisle.

Quirkily, owing to the change of railway company ownership, the mileages change at the aforementioned headshunt buffer stops: this point is both 12 miles and 5 chains (19.4km) from Bransty signal box but also 0 miles and 0 chains on the journey to Carlisle.

Wigton (WN)

Date Built	1957
LNWR Type or Builder	BR London Midland Type 15
No. of Levers	40
Ways of Working	AB
Current Status	Active
Listed (Y/N)	N

Wigton can trace its origins back to Roman times, and the town has developed into a thriving and attractive agricultural market centre.

The major employer in the town is Innovia, who started business life as British Rayothane and had a pair of sidings behind the station, which now appear to be disused. The town has produced at least two broadcasters of note – Melvyn Bragg, now ennobled and taking the title Lord Bragg of Wigton, and Anna Ford.

In Fig. 23 a class 156 two-car DMU hurries past Wigton signal box on its way to Carlisle. The siding leading to the British Rayothane works is on the extreme left. There is a ground frame released from the box to gain access to the siding about half a mile from the signal box.

Fig. 24 shows the layout from the fine station footbridge looking towards Maryport. The WN 37 signal has a chequered plate on the front that obliges any driver stopped at the signal to telephone the signal box. This requirement is often in place where the signal is not visible from the box or the track is not track circuited, but neither applies here.

In Fig. 25 the view is of the platforms looking towards Carlisle. The platform on the left has a ramp in the middle of it to enable wheelchairs better train access. Part of the platform construction is different where it acts as part of the road

Fig. 23   Wigton signal box, December 2014.

Fig. 24   Wigton looking towards Maryport, December 2014.

Fig. 25   Wigton looking towards Carlisle, December 2014.

overbridge at the end. The platform white edging does not venture this far, though.

Wigton station is 16 miles and 20 chains (26.2km) from Maryport, and control of the line now passes to Carlisle power signal box.

North Lancashire

The only two signal boxes in this region – Bare Lane and Hest Bank – were around the Morecambe Bay area.

Bare Lane (BL)

Date Built	1937
LNWR Type or Builder	LMS Type 11+
No. of Levers	32
Ways of Working	TCB, OTW, OTS
Current Status	Demolished January 2014
Listed (Y/N)	N

Bare Lane signal box controlled the branch off the West Coast Main Line that split into two to service the seaside resort of Morecambe and the ferry port (and later nuclear power station) at Heysham. The connection to Preston power box was worked track circuit block so there was no mechanical signalling here.

The box did have two types of single-line working: one train working without staff to Morecambe; and one train staff to Heysham.

Bare Lane to Morecambe – OTW

This is not a reference to trains running without people; rather the 'staff' is a piece of wood that acted as the authority to proceed in earlier days. The actual staff was dispensed with when track circuits came into use that denied access to another train if the branch line to Morecambe was occupied by a train.

There is a special override to enable a train to rescue another that has broken down in the OTW section but there are strict rules governing its use.

Morecambe has not fared well in terms of its rail connections and now has fairly basic facilities. It does, however, have the Midland Hotel, a splendid art deco structure opened by the LMS in 1933, which has recently been refurbished. Trains to Heysham have to first travel down the parallel single track to Morecambe, and if they are locomotive hauled, run round there before setting off for Heysham.

Bare Lane to Heysham – OTS

This way of working does involve a staff or token, and the staff can be divided into two or more sections and parts given to different trains. The parts can then be re-united into one staff, usually by screwing them together. The staff also has a metal key on the end which is used to unlock point levers at ground frames on the branch line. Staffs also bear the name of the branch line to which they relate, usually engraved on a brass plate, and redundant staffs are prized collector's items.

Fig. 26   Bare Lane signal box, May 2007.

Fig. 27   Bare Lane station house, May 2007.

Direct Rail Services operate nuclear flask trains to the power station and there is a passenger service to Heysham station itself. Although the station is advertised as Heysham Port, the ferry services appear to be freight only.

Fig. 26 is Bare Lane signal box with bricked-up locking frame windows and generally uPVC'd first floor but with a wooden staircase. The box also supervised the road crossing as well as the station gardens. Originally the void beneath the platform by the box would have contained point rodding and signal wires.

Bare Lane station was opposite the box, and the tracks in front of the station, seen in Fig. 27, are unusual. They are two single independent lines that both go to Morecambe, but as described above, one of the tracks goes eventually to Heysham with a branch off that to the power station. It is quite common for trains to travel alongside each other in the same direction although there is no suggestion of racing.

The station building featured in the BBC TV programme *Homes under the Hammer*.

Hest Bank Level Crossing Frame

Date Built	1958
LNWR Type or Builder	BR London Midland Region Type 15
No. of Levers	IFS panel
Ways of Working	TCB
Current Status	Closed
Listed (Y/N)	N

Originally Hest Bank had been a block post on the WCML and the place where the northern access to the Morecambe branch was controlled.

In 1912 there had been an incident that involved a goods train dividing in Hest Bank's section. The train had been checked at a signal, and when it set off it left fourteen wagons on the down main line. The signaller gave the Train out of Section bell code, which is 2 pause 1, to Carnforth without checking that the tail lamp was present. It was not, and a succeeding passenger train ran into the wagons, which had not been protected with detonators by the guard of the goods train. Miraculously there were no fatalities. Both individuals were carpeted.

The box at Hest Bank was later a gate box, supervising the road crossing, and is the only point at which Morecambe Bay or the West Coast can be viewed from a train on the WCML. The box also had an anemometer to measure wind speed, as it can be draughty across Morecambe Bay, and this can be seen above the name plate in Fig. 28. Morecambe Bay is in the background as well as the Cumbrian coast and Furness Railway territory. The box was

Fig. 28   Hest Bank Level Crossing Frame, August 2008.

equipped with an individual function switch panel and a separate panel to operate the crossing.

Control of Hest Bank's functionality passed to Preston power box in 2013.

Crewe to Shrewsbury

This journey travels from the railway hub Crewe, in south Cheshire, across rich farming country and meeting the Shropshire Union Canal, into north Shropshire. Several smaller towns are visited before reaching the county town of Shropshire, Shrewsbury. Whilst Crewe is almost the acme of modernity in railway signalling terms, Shrewsbury is a centre for semaphore signalling and signal boxes.

The journey would be very different today, with track circuit block and axle counters replacing the semaphore signalling absolute block section on the route described, although much of the Shrewsbury railway scene is still the same.

The simplified, not-to-scale diagram in Fig. 29 gives us an inkling of the complex nature of both Crewe and Shrewsbury in a railway context.

Axle counters relieve the signalling system of the requirement to signal Train out of Section for a train that has travelled through a section of track – a system we saw was wanting at Hest Bank in 1912, above. Axle counters are not a new idea as they were employed in the Severn Tunnel as long ago as 1991.

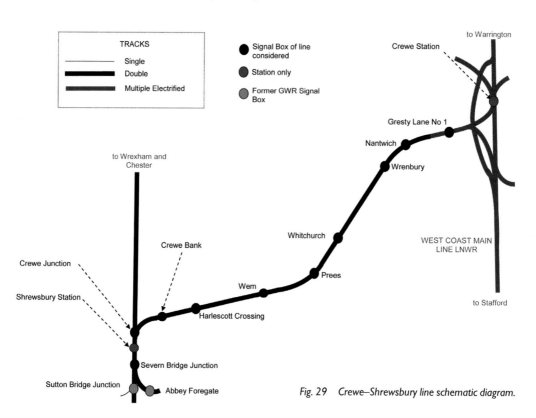

Fig. 29   Crewe–Shrewsbury line schematic diagram.

Fig. 30   Gresty Lane signal box, January 2015.

Gresty Lane No. 1 (GL)

Date Built	1889
LNWR Type or Builder	LNWR Type 4+
No. of Levers	IFS panel
Ways of Working	TCB, AB
Current Status	Active
Listed (Y/N)	N

Gresty Lane in Crewe is steeped in railway history from early times. There was an engine shed here belonging to the Great Western Railway, who had access to Crewe station via the Market Drayton and Wellington branch that ran into Nantwich, which is part of the journey we are travelling on. The GWR engine shed at Gresty Lane closed in around 1963 but former GWR engines still appeared on Crewe South freight (coded 5B) steam sheds for some time after that.

The site is an extensive junction and depot for rolling stock as well as DRS locomotives. The electrified tracks extend for about 1¼ miles (2km) alongside extensive sidings, of which there are fifteen on the western side alone.

Fig. 30 depicts a Gresty Lane No. 1 in the thick of it in terms of urban and railway environments. The box is at a junction of three double-track lines. The two main lines past the front of the box join the WCML via Crewe station from the left and head for Shrewsbury to the right. A double-track main line joins this formation before the box on the left,

termed the up and down Liverpool independent lines, and these bypass Crewe station and join the WCML. There are crossovers to the Manchester independent lines, which dive under the WCML to form the quadruple tracks to Sandbach, Stockport and Manchester Piccadilly.

The other double-track line passes to the rear of the box and comes from Crewe Sorting Sidings, which are much concerned with the movement of track materials – ballast, sleepers and rail. The box works permissive absolute block to Crewe Sorting Sidings North (*see* Crewe Sorting Sidings North in the Cheshire section later in this chapter). It also works AB to Salop Goods Junction.

The hipped roof buildings to the right of the box are the headquarters of Direct Rail Services. Behind

Fig. 31   Gresty Lane looking towards Shrewsbury, January 2015.

Fig. 32   *Gresty Lane looking towards Crewe station and junctions, January 2015.*

Nantwich (NH)

Date Built	1948
LNWR Type or Builder	LMS Type 11c
No. of Levers	30
Ways of Working	AB
Current Status	Closed
Listed (Y/N)	N

the box is a DRS Compass-liveried class 66 on a permanent way train.

In Fig. 31 Gresty Lane No. 1 signal box and the DRS depot are prepared for winter, with the snow plough in view as well as a line of locomotives. They appear to be a couple of class 47/57 and what looks like some of the more modern class 68.

The signal box is behind the camera in Fig. 32, which shows two of the double-track lines. The nearer is the Liverpool independent line and the further, with the class 175 Coradia DMU on it, runs from Crewe station heading for Shrewsbury. The leading car is 175 008. The final pair of tracks from Crewe yards is hidden behind the saplings.

Fig. 33 shows the box from the rear to show those other tracks from the yards. Class 66, 66623 Bill Bolsover, makes off towards Shrewsbury with a ballast train.

Nantwich has been part of the Cheshire salt-producing area for about 1,000 years. Today it is a delightful and pretty town that is a centre for the historically well-off Cheshire farming community, with many fine half-timbered buildings – some of which date from the sixteenth century.

There had been four other signal boxes in and around Nantwich and this one was originally Nantwich Station; it is still so named on the box but is not called that officially. The box in Fig. 34 still has what looks like original-style locking frame windows as well as the cock's comb ridge tiles. It was originally Wem North, which was further down this line.

There has been a move to preserve the box by the Reverend Malcolm Lorimer, who is a Methodist minister in the town. The clergy is quite often involved with railways, and the Rev. Teddy Boston, Rev. Wilbert Awdry, Rev. Peter Denny and the Bishop of Wakefield, Eric Treacy, have all been prominent in various railway fields. The Rev. Lorimer plans to remove the box to his church, which already has a miniature railway running

Fig. 33   *Rear of Gresty Lane signal box, January 2015.*

round it. The Reverend also has his own website and is an author.

Fig. 35 shows Nantwich signal box looking towards Wrenbury. Shortly the line crosses the River Weaver, which we shall next meet again when we go to Frodsham, where the Weaver flows into Mersey Estuary. After the river the line crosses the Shropshire Union Canal, which at this point is making its way from Market Drayton to Ellesmere Port on the Mersey. There is no point rodding coming from the box, and the trailing crossover just north of the station is provided with a ground frame. Such a crossover is only operated in an emergency if there is a blockage on one of the lines.

Nantwich station has not only a station building but a footbridge as well, which can be used by pedestrians when the level crossing barriers are down. Fig. 36 is a view from the footbridge and of the reasonably complete station building looking towards Crewe. The building is a restaurant at the survey date and the passengers are provided with a brick and concrete-roofed shelter in ARP style. There has been some gardening here but the piece of track, which is a point frog component, must get in the way.

Albrecht Discounts occupy part of where the goods shed and yard used to be. South of here was the junction with the Market Drayton and Wellington line and so Nantwich would have been much busier than it is now. The platform starter signal has a sighting board that retains a gap to enable the signaller to see the tell-tale rearward-facing light of the signal arm. When this light is covered up by the arc-shaped metal piece at the rear of the signal it means the arm has been raised to clear, or gone 'off'. The arc-shaped piece is referred to as a backlight cover or blinder.

'Waiting for the off' was a commonly used phrase at one time and it is thought to derive from a train waiting for the signal to proceed, although there are horse racing connotations as well.

Nantwich signal box is 4 miles 19 chains (6.8km) from Crewe South Junction.

Fig. 34   Nantwich signal box, October 2004.

Fig. 35   Nantwich signal box looking towards Shrewsbury, October 2004.

Fig. 36   Nantwich station looking towards Crewe, October 2004.

Wrenbury (WY)

Date Built	1882
LNWR Type or Builder	LNWR Type 4+
No. of Levers	17
Ways of Working	AB
Current Status	Closed
Listed (Y/N)	N

Wrenbury is a charming village whose centre is a conservation area, and there are a good many listed buildings there. It sees many visitors in the summer months from canal boat holidaymakers who are travelling the Shropshire Union Canal – not the same part as at Nantwich, but the branch to Llangollen, reputedly the most popular part of the entire canal system. The canal has three of Thomas Telford's cantilever lifting bridges over the canal, dating from 1790; you have to pull on a rope to get them to lift but because they are counterbalanced it is not difficult.

A favourite haunt of travellers and locals is the Dusty Miller Inn right on the canal bank; close by, in close competition, is the Cotton Arms. Both are renowned for their food and canal boat-friendliness.

The signal box at Wrenbury in Fig. 37 is quite mature, and this usually means there haven't been many changes over the years. Wrenbury, in common with many other places, lost its goods yard. The goods shed remains, as does a domestic coal yard. However, the box is in fairly original condition except for windows and steps.

Fig. 38 shows the signal box looking towards Whitchurch. Despite it being a wet and miserable day, the home signal shows up well with the whitewashed bridge background. The other home signal, for the Crewe direction, is expecting a class 150 two-car unit, which were staples at the time of the survey. Note the hoops on the signal levers inside the box. The London and North Western was unusual in that signallers grabbed the hoop to release the latch in the frame to make a pull, rather than grabbing the shiny top of the lever and then hold the latch lever in. The barrier control panel

Fig. 37 Wrenbury signal box, October 2004.

Fig. 38 Wrenbury looking towards Shrewsbury, October 2004.

Fig. 39 Wrenbury station, October 2004.

is by the window. These crossings are supervised from Cardiff now.

Wrenbury retains part of the station building, although it is in private hands and the information sign advertises a local brewery (Fig. 39). This is a somewhat recurrent theme on the journey, as Wem has been renowned locally for breweries since the nineteenth century.

Wrenbury station is 8 miles and 48 chains (13.8km) from Crewe South Junction.

Whitchurch (WH)

Date Built	1897
LNWR Type or Builder	LNWR Type 4
No. of Levers	55
Ways of Working	AB
Current Status	Demolished
Listed (Y/N)	N

We leave Cheshire for the first stop in Shropshire, and as an English place name Whitchurch is right up there with Stoke, Norton and Newport in the popularity stakes. The town's function as a stopping place on the Roman road from Chester to Wroxeter ensured it an early place in the history books. Despite being mostly an agricultural marketplace, the town is also famous for Joyce's clocks, which have graced public buildings and stations for many years – the company dates from 1690 and they even had a hand in Big Ben. The town merits a branch off the Shropshire Union Canal as well as the Grindley Brook staircase locks.

The town is only about 3 miles (5km) from the Welsh border and the line is dubbed the Welsh Marches Line.

As a railway town Whitchurch was quite a junction in former days with one end of the Manchester and Milford Railway, which went to neither place, but ended up as the Cambrian Railways and ultimately a constituent of the GWR.

There was also a branch line cross country via Malpas to Chester. This was handy for avoiding Crewe and was used by some passenger trains at busy times. It was also a route for Welsh coal during World War I.

Whitchurch signal box was last regularly used during the 1990s, with the last recorded activity in 2008. The box looks ready for the wrecking ball in 2004, in Fig. 40. Clearly it was a cut above the normal box on the branch and a lofty vantage point as well as having a high lever count. The box was switched out in later years, so that if the block bell was operated in Wrenbury it would ring in Prees, the next box along, and all signals here were permanently off, or clear. The switching out was achieved by a large wooden box with brass fittings that could have been an exhibit at the Victoria and Albert Museum but contained a number of electrical switches that bypassed the box's electrical functions that controlled the absolute block instruments.

Fig. 41 illustrates some of the former grandeur of Whitchurch station, with a large retaining wall on the left that supported an overall roof; the bay platform is still visible but there are no tracks there. The original cast iron columns support the much later girders and corrugated iron roof. The goods shed is on the far left behind the wall and is now a garage. The birch trees on the right conceal the remains of much trackwork. The view is towards Crewe with the box in the distance, past the colour light signal.

Fig. 40   Whitchurch signal box, November 2004.

Fig. 41   Whitchurch station looking towards Crewe, November 2004.

Fig. 42   Prees signal box, November 2004.

Whitchurch station is 13 miles and 44 chains (21.8km) from Crewe South Junction.

Prees (PS)

Date Built	1881
LNWR Type or Builder	LNWR Type 4
No. of Levers	25
Ways of Working	AB
Current Status	Closed
Listed (Y/N)	N

The rich agricultural farmland of north Shropshire continues towards Shrewsbury and the attractive small town of Prees. The railway fortunes of Prees were shaped by a Captain Black, who insisted that the railway run no less than a mile from his mill in Mill Street, where it still is today. The Shropshire Union Canal has a branch known as the Prees branch that ends up at Whixall marina, a popular spot with canal boaters. There had been a branch off the line to service an army camp at Prees Heath, which later became RAF Tilstock.

Apart from the windows and steps the box in Fig. 42 is remarkably original after 130 years in service.

Fig. 43 shows a class 150 approaching from the Crewe direction in 2004. In 2015 the class 175 Coradia units are doing about 70mph (110km/h) at this point and passengers are entreated to flag the train down. It seems unlikely that they would

Fig. 43   Prees station looking towards Crewe, November 2004.

be able to pull up to the platform in time unless the units have been fitted with thrust reversers, brake parachutes and possibly drag chains. Perhaps there is a case for passenger-operated distant signals that are controlled by the bar code on the passenger's ticket and reset by the passage of the train. The box looks just the same after closure but has no frame or instruments within.

The rear of the signal box is shown in Fig. 44. It is slightly strange that there is no rear window as the road curves around at this point and a window would help to gauge the traffic situation. However, the road is very lightly used.

Prees station is 18 miles and 36 chains (29.7km) from Crewe South Junction.

Wem (WM)

Date Built	1883
LNWR Type or Builder	LNWR Type 4+
No. of Levers	35
Ways of Working	AB
Current Status	Closed
Listed (Y/N)	N

Wem is an attractive market town as well as a local administrative centre. It is also the place where the sweet pea flower was commercially developed by a Scotsman named Henry Eckford.

Small-scale brewing of beer took place here for hundreds of years, which eventually expanded to a brewery that occupied prominent premises in Wem until 1988. The tradition continues with the Hanby micro brewery.

Fig. 45 shows Wem signal box looking largely original except for the windows. There is point rodding emerging from the box so there was some extra track here in addition to the double running lines. Unlike Prees, the box is right in the middle of town and busy with traffic. The box looks as though the coal stove was at the front, judging by the newer roof slates and the position of what appears to be a gas flue.

Fig. 46 is looking towards Shrewsbury and the down refuge siding. There is no ground disc to signal a reversing move into the siding so perhaps it was done with hand signals from the box, flags or Bardic lamp. The ground disc to come out is visible, complete with backlight. The trap point position means that any vehicles reversing into the siding must be clear of the trap point before the point can be changed to the running line.

Fig. 44   Rear of Prees signal box, November 2004.

Fig. 45   Wem signal box, November 2004.

Fig. 46   Wem looking towards Shrewsbury, November 2004.

Fig. 47 Wem station looking towards Shrewsbury, November 2004.

Looking towards Prees and Crewe in Fig. 47, you can see some attempt to garden, with evergreens in the raised beds; perhaps there are sweet peas in spring.

The bracketed-out colour light signal is momentarily in sync with the road barrier lights but the barriers themselves are yet to fall.

Wem station is 21 miles and 57 chains (34.9km) from Crewe South Junction.

The line continues to Yorton, which has a station building in the style of Wrenbury and a charming brick-built waiting room on the down side towards Crewe. The signal box and signalling were removed some years ago.

Yorton station is 25 miles and 14 chains (40.5km) from Crewe South Junction.

Harlescott Crossing (HT)

Date Built	c.1882
LNWR Type or Builder	LNWR Type 4+
No. of Levers	38
Ways of Working	AB
Current Status	Closed
Listed (Y/N)	N

Harlescott, now a suburb of Shrewsbury, once held the town's extensive cattle market, which suffered after the 2001 foot-and-mouth outbreak, although there is still a livestock market in the area. Harlescott is now busy with retail, leisure and light industry.

The signal box at Harlescott is shown in Fig. 48, and at least one of the signallers is clearly a

Fig. 48 Harlescott Crossing signal box, Shrewsbury, November 2004.

Fig. 49   Harlescott Crossing looking towards Shrewsbury, November 2004.

gardener and birdwatcher. The characterful cross-ing keeper's cottage has been sold off but the box continues in railway service and has lasted for about 130 years. The home signal is exceptionally tall for sighting purposes. The box was extended in 1941 to serve a group of sidings that were built for the military. The windows are irregular widths that bear testament to the alterations, as does the fact that there are only two locking frame room window ledges on the ground floor – an oddity that appears to be repeated around the rear of the building.

The signal box has a railway customer in the shape of a class 153 on its way to Crewe in Fig. 49. This 2004 scene updated would be a class 175 Coradia twin unit, but the box remains, at least for the time being.

Some side and rear detail of the signal box are shown in Fig. 50. The cottage vegetable garden is right up against the box; often parts of the line side would be used as allotments by signallers or station staff in the days when there were some. Since the box closed there have been problems with the new signalling system and an already busy road cross-ing has become gridlocked at times.

Harlescott Crossing signal box is 30 miles 29 chains (48.9km) from Crewe South Junction.

Further down, the line passes the site of the Sentinel Waggon (*sic*) Works who manufactured steam-powered lorries, railway locomotives, and later, diesel-engined lorries and locomotives. Some of the last diesel-engined locomotives were shunt-ers for the Manchester Ship Canal with Rolls-Royce engines, and the company had been acquired by the prestigious engine manufacturer by 1966. There is a survivor of this class on the Bluebell Railway.

Fig. 50   Rear of Harlescott Crossing signal box, November 2004.

Crewe Bank (CB)

Date Built	1943
LNWR Type or Builder	LMS Type 11c
No. of Levers	30
Ways of Working	AB
Current Status	Closed
Listed (Y/N)	N

Coming into Shrewsbury now, we pass the site of the Flax Mill (known as The Maltings subsequently) at Ditherington, which is the oldest iron-framed building in the world and Grade I listed. It is said to be the father of all skyscraper buildings and was completed in 1797.

Crewe Bank signal box was another wartime expedient (Fig. 51) and its construction reflects the requirement to withstand blast from bombing in

Fig. 51   Crewe Bank signal box, Shrewsbury, July 2014.

World War II, after closure. Note the concrete posts and panels forming and framing the steps. What is remarkable is that even when the nation was facing annihilation someone thought to decorate the brickwork with two bands of engineer's blue facing bricks.

As well as being a block post to Crewe Junction, just by Shrewsbury station, it also controlled a goods loop on the up side towards Shrewsbury and a group of sidings that were Smallshaw's coal merchant's premises. Their address is still given as LMS New Yard, Castle Foregate, Shrewsbury.

Shrewsbury Crewe Bank signal box, as it was sometimes known, is shown in earlier days in Fig. 52 and notionally still in service, as we can see from the name plate. The box was switched out for years but was switched in when the early steam specials used to call here in the 1970s.

Early steam specials were confined to a few routes, one of which was the Welsh border line between Hereford, Shrewsbury and Chester. The engines would be placed in the goods loop here and a hose run over the fence from a Shropshire Fire and Rescue Service fire engine. Their headquarters is just by the black fence, out of shot on the left.

Speaking of the fence, it is a typical railway product made of slices of old timber sleepers held together with wire and then painted with black gas tar. The goods loop starter is the taller of the two signals and the view is towards Crewe Junction and Shrewsbury station.

The home signal on the other side of the track is controlled by Crewe Junction but slotted by Crewe Bank. This means that because of the closeness of the boxes to each other, Crewe Bank must agree to pull off to enable this Crewe Junction signal to be pulled off. This kind of inter-box interlock is known as 'slotting' and the mechanism is on the signal post.

As Crewe Bank is switched out and pulled off, it only requires Crewe Junction to pull off to lift the signal arm.

Just to the right of this home signal in the distance is a pair of sighting boards next to each other at about the same level as the signal arm described above, and these are two ex-GWR or rather Western Region home signals from the Chester line, so the junction is not far away. Worthy of note are the older-style yard lamps.

Fig. 52   Crewe Bank signal box approaches to Shrewsbury, September 2005.

Fig. 53 (left)   Crewe Bank, Shrewsbury, from the Crewe direction, September 2005.

Fig. 54 (above)   Updated Crewe Bank signalling, July 2014.

Fig. 53 shows Shrewsbury Crewe Bank signal CB 26 on the bracket and lattice post. This signal is the up home for trains towards Shrewsbury so we are looking back to Harlescott Crossing, just over a mile (1.5km) away, and Crewe. The distant would be Crewe Junction's if it was controllable but it is fixed at caution, which explains why there is no green lens on the arm: it is never off so it doesn't need one. The signal in the distance is Crewe Bank's down outer home and the Crewe Bank box is behind the camera.

Our final view of Crewe Bank is Fig. 54, and this is ten years after the other pictures. The spotty-looking object with the red LEDs is a modern signal from the experimental signalling now in use on the line. Crewe Junction's outer home that we saw at a distance in Fig. 52 has been modernized but remains. The coal yard machinery is visible beyond the purple buddleia and beyond that is the pair of lower quadrant signals from the Chester line that we glimpsed before, and even further beyond that are the Welsh hills.

Crewe Bank signal box is 31 miles 79 chains (51.5km) from Crewe South Junction.

The following two signal boxes were covered in the GWR volume in this series as Shrewsbury was a joint LNWR/GWR station. However, the treatment here is different and no photographs are duplicated.

Crewe Junction (CJ)

Date Built	1903
LNWR Type or Builder	LNWR Type 4
No. of Levers	120
Ways of Working	AB
Current Status	Active
Listed (Y/N)	Y

Crewe Junction is by far the largest ex-LNWR box encountered so far and it still mostly does what it was designed to do over 110 years ago. The box supervises the northern half of Shrewsbury station as well as the junction between the Chester and Crewe lines, and as most of the lines may have a need to go to most of the platforms, the junction is still a complex one.

The box in Fig. 55 is large and in very good condition, as befits its status as a listed building. The box is

situated off the north end of platform 3. The signals involved are GWR/Western Region pattern lower quadrants, LMS/London Midland Region upper quadrant semaphores and colour light signals, some with route indicators. The signal apparently to the left-hand side of the box is a lower quadrant with subsidiary calling on arm. The purpose of the calling on arm is to signal a train into a platform where a train may already be standing. The train is brought to a stand and then the calling on arm is lowered off, which advises the driver to proceed with the utmost caution. In addition to calling on arms a number of signals are equipped with 'stencil boxes' that may qualify the calling on. A 'C' denotes proceed with caution to platform where there may be a train already; and an 'S' means clear to shunt only, for example adding another coach to a set in past times.

Although Crewe Junction appears squat from the railway side, at street level it is actually a very tall building (*see* Fig. 56). The LNWR apparently had to build them this tall to accommodate the locking equipment. There is a piece later in this chapter where this very feature helped to cause a problem on the LMS (*see* Lichfield Trent Valley No. 1).

The Midland's compact lever frame won out and led to it being adopted as standard for the LMS and London Midland Region of BR. Shrewsbury

station is very much built up compared with street level, mainly to span the River Severn. Shrewsbury station cost £170,000 to build, a fortune in relative terms, and is a treasured architectural gem.

In Fig. 57 the camera is looking at the signal box on the end of platform 3 down the Chester line. The double-track main line heads off under the road bridge and the third line gives access to Coton Hill goods yard, which is just about surviving. The

Fig. 56   Rear of Shrewsbury Crewe Junction signal box, July 2014.

Fig. 57   Shrewsbury looking towards Chester, January 2015.

entry to the platforms is guarded by the two sets of bracket signals – the one further away is the one we saw at Crewe Bank in Fig. 53 and the nearer one has calling on arms and stencil boxes. The one further away also has two elevated ground discs by the side of it and this is to signal the exit from the Coton Hill yard. The large brick building behind the nearer bracket was Castle Foregate goods shed, which is now given over to retail and light industrial units, although some trackwork and railway features remain.

Fig. 58 shows Crewe Junction signal box's position relative to Shrewsbury station. The gantry only has three posts or dolls but you can easily see where the remains of four more posts are. Originally there were ten dolls on this gantry. This was a favourite

place to pose steam locomotives, and as Crewe Works sent all its Pacifics and top locomotives down the Crewe–Shrewsbury line for a workout, GWR and LMS express passenger locomotives would often be pictured here together.

The signal under-slung from the canopy roof on platform 4 is a banner repeater, and it is repeating what signal CJ 97 is doing on the gantry. CJ 97 can't be seen directly at all times from platform 4 so the banner relays the status of the signal but not the route. The track in the middle is the down main line to Chester and was much used by freight trains, so it is to be hoped its kit form appearance is only temporary.

Crewe Junction 9, or CJ 9, is the first signal encountered off the Crewe line after Crewe Bank

Fig. 58   Shrewsbury station looking towards Chester and Crewe, January 2015.

Fig. 59 Crewe Junction signal off the Crewe line towards Shrewsbury station, January 2015.

(Fig. 59). The three arms are for choice of line: from left to right, up main freight avoiding line, platform 7 and platform 4. The Coradia is headed for platform 7. The telephone number on the post is Crewe Junction's and train drivers can call the box on the

GSM-R mobile phone system if held at a signal. GSM is the Global System for Mobile Communications and is the prevalent digital mobile phone technology in Europe and the USA.

Fig. 60 is looking back down the Crewe line. Signal CJ 9, which we saw in Fig. 59, is down the line a bit around the curve on the right. The three single post signals control the lines that the up main line splits into from Crewe to come into the platforms or take the avoiding line at the back of the station. They all have calling on arms and stencil boxes. The bracket on the left is for the Chester line.

In Fig. 61 a class 175 Coradia DMU coming from Chester has been checked by the signaller, bringing the train almost to a stand before pulling off the board where the DMU is in the photo. It is the right-hand signal on the far bracket and the arm has dropped below the sighting board so it is invisible. If it had been the left-hand arm, as we look at it, the train would have been destined for platform 4, opposite the box. As it is, it can go either to platform 7 or the goods avoiding line at the back of the station. The next bracket tells us it is platform 7. Note that the second bracket's signals are of

Fig. 60 Crewe Junction looking towards Crewe line, January 2015.

Fig. 61   Crewe Junction and signal box, January 2015.

different heights and this means the lower is to be taken at a lower speed. There are also roundel-type speed restriction signs to advise drivers.

Fig. 62 shows platform 7 at Shrewsbury station, with the London Midland Region upper quadrant signal, CJ 53, expecting a train; the point is set for the Crewe line. A class 150 hurries off towards Chester. The freight avoiding line is to the right of the signal post and there is alternative access to it from the Crewe line. The 7464 1501 on the brick pillar on the left and seen on other signals is the mobile number that a driver has to dial to contact Crewe Junction signal box (typically if brought to a stand at a signal).

The signaller can also dial the train driver and issue commands. The system is a specialized form of digital mobile network where trains and signal boxes have their numbers allocated and the system must know which service a train is operating on a particular day. This system replaced the national radio system, which was an early attempt to have signaller-to-driver communications, which in turn replaced signal post phones.

Crewe Junction signal box is 32 miles 25 chains (52km) from Crewe South Junction and 171 miles 57 chains (276.3km) from London Paddington via Oxford and Birmingham Snow Hill.

Fig. 62   Shrewsbury station platform 7, July 2014.

Severn Bridge Junction (SBJ)

Date Built	1903
LNWR Type or Builder	LNWR Type 4
No. of Levers	180
Ways of Working	AB
Current Status	Active
Listed (Y/N)	Y

Fig. 63   Severn Bridge Junction signal box, January 2015.

Just as 180 is the top score in a game of darts, so it is with signal boxes. Shrewsbury Severn Bridge Junction is now the largest mechanical signal box in the world and needs two signallers on a daytime shift to cope with the traffic movements.

The situation is even more complicated than the north end of Shrewsbury station in that there are two more platforms to be considered, as well as the carriage sidings and a double-track main line behind the box. There are two basic destinations from Severn Bridge Junction: Wolverhampton via Wellington (Shropshire); or Hereford, with a further branch off to the Cambrian main line.

The box appears cathedral-like in Fig. 63 and seems to dwarf Shrewsbury Abbey in the background. The line to Wolverhampton goes off to the

left and to Hereford to the right. Behind the box is a double-track main line that joins the two and is used mostly for freight working, as it avoids the station completely. The principal source of freight traffic is imported coal from Avonmouth to Midlands power stations. The Shrewsbury name plate is advice to passengers, as at Crewe Junction, and the box's name is on a smaller plate beneath the walkway. As at Crewe Junction, there is also a modernized fire escape ladder but the main way up to the operating room is by internal staircase.

Fig. 64 is a more panoramic view of Severn Bridge Junction's area of control. From the left is a siding known as the Howard Street Landing. This is not an oblique reference to a BBC drama series of the 1980s but named after the street next to the station that contains Shrewsbury Prison – a fine 18th-century building built by the prison reformer John Howard and Thomas Telford. The building vies for admiration with the Butter Market in the same street. There are well over 600 listed buildings in Shrewsbury, spanning an extraordinary variety of ages and styles from medieval times onwards.

This siding now appears disused and the cross-over to release engines is in the course of removal.

Next is the freight avoiding line referred to above under Crewe Junction, then platforms 7, 6, 5 and 4. After that comes the other freight avoiding line and finally platform 3. Platforms 1 and 2 used to accommodate the branch trains to Kidderminster on the extreme right, part of which is now the Severn Valley Railway. Some years later these platforms were a makeshift workshop where Vale of Rheidol coaches were restored, in the days when the V of R belonged to British Railways.

The class 175 Coradia departing from platform 7 is taking the Hereford line and the ex-GWR centre-balanced lower quadrant signal is its permission to proceed. The London Midland Region upper quadrant is for the freight avoiding line which seems a

Fig. 64   Severn Bridge Junction signal box and the south of Shrewsbury station, January 2015.

bit odd as signals are supposed to be on the left of the line they refer to, but it must be a sighting issue. Note that towards the bottom right of the picture the guard of a train is advised that the signal was off by the illuminated sign, so the canopy must be in the way of a line of sight. This is another form of repeater signal that we saw with the banner at the other end of the station.

The canopy itself is a relatively modern innovation from the 1960s – prior to that the station had an overall roof.

Platforms 6 and 5 both have colour light signals with route indicators and platform 4 has the LMR bracket signal. Shrewsbury passed to the LMR in 1963 but only parts of the station have been converted to upper quadrant signals.

Fig. 65 is more or less the same view again except that attention focuses on the London Midland class 170 DMU hiding underneath the canopy in platform 6. The colour light signal, partially obscured, has turned to green and the route indicator says W for Wolverhampton.

In Fig. 66 the departure is complete and the colour light has already turned red and extinguished the route indicator display; these actions are automatic as the train passes the signal head rather than manual with semaphores. This is why two pictures were needed to illustrate the move. A Coradia DMU arrives from Hereford into platform 4 on the right. The two departures and one arrival took place within three minutes.

Fig. 67 takes a look at some more of Severn Bridge Junction's signals with a view towards the Hereford line and Sutton Bridge Junction, where the Cambrian splits off for Aberystwyth and Pwllheli.

The colour light signal on platform 5 is almost by the LMR bracket at the end of platform 4. Beyond that is an upper quadrant (SBJ 23), the shorter of two signals on the left, and this is to hold a down train that has run around the back of the box before it joins the line to Hereford. The taller lower quadrant (SBJ 22) is to hold a down train that has left platform 7 from going to Hereford. The off status of these two signals must be mutually exclusive in the sense that both could not be off at the same time as

Fig. 65   Severn Bridge Junction signal box and the south of Shrewsbury station with Wolverhampton departure, part 1, January 2015.

Fig. 66   Severn Bridge Junction signal box and the south of Shrewsbury station with Wolverhampton departure, part 2, January 2015.

Fig. 67   Shrewsbury station looking towards Sutton Bridge Junction, January 2015.

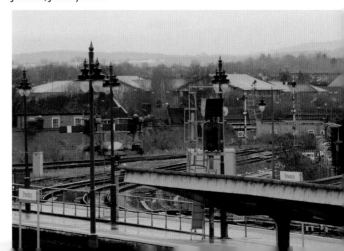

Fig. 68 Severn Bridge Junction signal box from the Wolverhampton direction, July 2014.

their routes would conflict. This is arranged in the mechanical locking inside the box.

Beyond this is a home and distant lower quadrant signal on the same post on a slight curve but accentuated by the long-range camera shot. This signal belongs to Sutton Bridge Junction, the next box along the line. It is also the junction for the Cambrian line and the practice is to leave the distant on, as here, to caution a train that it is to take the slower Cambrian line at the junction. Clearly a Cambrian-bound train is expected.

Fig. 68 is a view from the Wolverhampton line towards Severn Bridge Junction. The lines on the far left are one track behind the box to the Hereford line used by freight trains. The two bracket signals of a three-arm (SBJ 124) and two-arm type (SBJ 74)

leading to the station have the following functions, from left to right:

1. Shrewsbury station platform 3
2. Down main or freight line, currently in bits – but the faster line
3. Shrewsbury station platform 4
4. Shrewsbury station platform 5
5. Shrewsbury station platform 6.

The left-hand upper quadrant with its back to us and the other upper quadrant on a bracket are Abbey Foregate signals, whose ex-GWR box is behind the camera.

Fig. 69 is the final view at Severn Bridge Junction, looking back from the box towards Shrewsbury station.

On the extreme left is the bay for platforms 1 and 2 as described earlier, and just by there are the supports, painted one shade of grey, for the overall roof removed in the 1960s. Platform 3 on the left has its own starter signal, as all platforms except 5 and 6 are bi-directionally signalled. The four-car class 150 series DMU has arrived from Wolverhampton and two of the cars are being detached and sent on.

The through freight road is looking poorly, with some track panels removed.

Platform 6 has the London Midland class 170 – 170 511 – which was mentioned above in the section about Fig. 68.

Fig. 69 Shrewsbury station looking north, January 2015.

The whole thing is presided over by the magnificent Tudor-esque station building and Shrewsbury Castle. The footbridge leads to Howard Street and HMP Shrewsbury and the Butter Market on the right.

At the far end of the platform is the gantry and Crewe Junction.

Severn Bridge Junction signal box is 171 miles and 33 chains (275.9km) from London Paddington via Oxford and Birmingham Snow Hill.

The joint LNWR/GWR continues to Hereford but there are no more LNWR signal boxes or signalling on that route.

Crewe to Chester and Holyhead

The journey this time is one of contrasts, in terms of scenery and infrastructure, as it follows one of the oldest routes, the ferry route to Ireland. The Irish Mail train first ran in 1848 and still runs to this day. The route, as shown in Fig. 70, crosses the Cheshire plain to the ancient and beautiful city of Chester, across the River Dee and along the estuary. It then mostly follows the coast with hills and mountains as an inland backdrop to the River Conway. Here there are two branches to Llandudno and Blaenau Ffestiniog. The line then continues to Bangor,

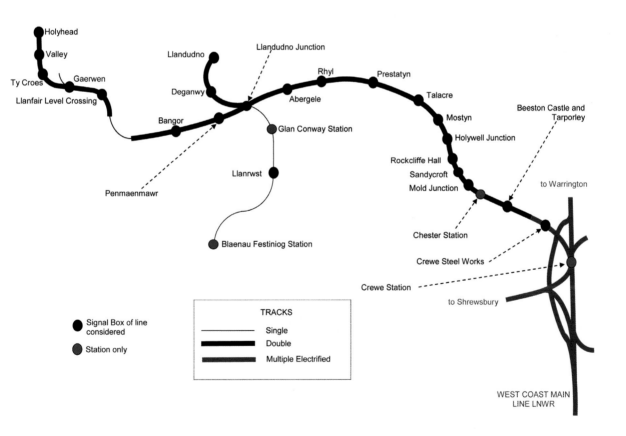

Fig. 70   Crewe–Chester and Holyhead line schematic diagram.

Fig. 71   Crewe Steel Works signal box, December 2014.

crosses the Menai Strait to Anglesey and then crosses that green isle to the port of Holyhead. The journey of about 100 miles (160km) is rich in London and North Western Railway history, and some of it is still in operation with the modern railway.

Crewe Steel Works (SW)

Date Built	1935
LNWR Type or Builder	LMS Type 11c
No. of Levers	20
Ways of Working	TCB, AB
Current Status	Active
Listed (Y/N)	N

Crewe Steel Works stands opposite what is now Bombardier Transportation, which had been part of Crewe locomotive works. The box controls entry to Crewe Electric Loco Depot, which has class 67, 90, 92 and 325 units allocated to it. There is a trailing crossover outside the box and the box works TCB to Crewe power box and AB to Beeston Castle and Tarporley, using an original LNWR block instrument.

Fig. 71 shows a box that has had to adapt from the steam age to a more modern era. The mesh grilling is standard in 25kV electric overhead areas and in this case seems to be a kind of safety cage for the walkway. Crewe was a target for the Luftwaffe in World War II, hence the bricked-up locking frame room windows. Note the red and white chequer enamel sign announcing 'Warning Limited Clearance'. The lever frame faces the rear wall inside the box.

Fig. 72 is looking towards Crewe station. An unusual aspect of the signalling here, although there isn't much of it, is the use of facing point locks on a trailing crossover and on the crossover into the electric depot, and it is completely track circuited. This is because passenger trains were run by the LMS into what was then part of Crewe works for staff that had been made redundant by the closure of the North Staffordshire Railways works at Stoke-on-Trent. These trains continued into BR days, and the signal box diagram labels the track beyond the point in Fig. 72 as 'carriage sidings'. No doubt staff made their way from there to the works across the track, and as railway employees their journeys would be free.

Some idea of the scale of the works can be seen from the building on the left – Crewe works employed up to 20,000 people at its peak.

The yellow mile post is on the right of the tracks and after the box but before the electric depot point. It announces 159 and two black circles, which means that the location is 159 miles and 40 chains (256.7km) from London Euston station. The electric overhead power supply finishes at 159 miles and 55 chains (257km) on the way to Chester. The first red colour light signal on the up side towards Crewe is slotted by Crewe power box, meaning the power box has to pull off as well as Crewe Steel Works for it to go off, or clear. The next red colour light belongs to Crewe power box.

Fig. 72   Crewe Steel Works signal box looking towards Crewe station, December 2014.

Fig. 73 (above)   Crewe Steel Works signal box rodding detail, December 2014.

Fig. 74 (right)   Crewe Steel Works signal box interior, December 2014.

A bit of detail outside the signal box is shown in Fig. 73. Starting at the bottom of the picture, the cranked rod that runs parallel with the rails for a bit is the facing-point lock rod. The point tie bar is the flat iron oxide-coloured piece of steel that joins both point blades. It has two slots cut into it, only one of which is visible. The facing-point lock is engaged into the slot we can't see at the moment. If the crossover needs to be changed over, first the facing-point lock must be withdrawn, with a blue lever in the box reversed, and this leaves the point tie bar to be moved to the new position. When the point has moved to the new position the facing-point lock is engaged in the slot we can presently see, which has itself moved over. The facing-point lock lever is then replaced to lock the tie bar in the new position.

Attached to the right-hand point blade is a further piece of flat bar that heads towards the box. This too has slots cut into it, and the two iron oxide-coloured boxes that are parallel to the right-hand rail have locating pieces that can engage with the slots cut into the flat bar. These are detection slides that will only permit the ground discs we saw in Fig. 72 to move to a new position if the point to which they refer has already moved to that new position. This is an example of a point and signal interlock that takes place outside the locking frame in the box. Point rodding was originally round and moved to a rectangular form later. You can see both types in use.

The yellow flat bars between the point blades are stretcher bars to maintain the gauge on the point blades. The other yellow object is a part of a ramp and cover that was commonly used to cover facing-point lock assemblies. These were used in the days when rolling stock had screw link couplings, which were adjustable in length. There were incidents when a coupling hanging loose while a train was in motion ripped up the facing-point mechanism, causing the blades to move and derail the train.

Fig. 74 gives a glimpse inside the signal box. The diagram shows a simple layout of basically two crossovers, all of which is track circuited. The gradient diagram inset into the diagram shows a fairly level line. The white light is signal diagram power on. On the block shelf are three black boxes stacked one on the other. They are train protection and warning system (TPWS) power supply and test indicators. TPWS exists to apply the brakes on a train that has passed a signal at danger (SPAD) or is speeding. At the end of the block shelf is the LNWR block instrument, which is used to communicate with Beeston Castle and Tarporley signal box. In the standard LMS frame, lever 10 is the facing point lock we saw at track level in Fig. 73, while lever 12 actually operates the point blades. Lever 9 operates the electric depot point, which is actually a crossover, including the headshunt. This uses facing-point lock levers (FPLs) 8 and 10, the same as the crossover, which means that the crossover must be in the running line or normal position before the electric depot crossover can be changed over. This is obviously highly desirable, as a train leaving the depot would derail on the crossover if it were to be permitted to be in opposition.

The lights hanging down from the block shelf are colour light signal status indicators; they can be used for semaphore signals although there aren't any here.

Beeston Castle and Tarporley (BC)

Date Built	1915
LNWR Type or Builder	LNWR Type 5+
No. of Levers	26
Ways of Working	AB
Current Status	Active
Listed (Y/N)	N

Fig. 75   Beeston Castle and Tarporley signal box, December 2014.

Into the delightful Cheshire countryside and Beeston Castle itself sits on a 350ft (100m) hill in the middle of the Cheshire plain and is visible for miles around, while the view from the castle is said to encompass eight counties on a clear day. Beeston itself was famous as a large cattle market centre until recent times.

Tarporley, on the other hand, is a popular and delightful large village, but at 2 miles (3km) from the former station, it was a bit of a hike. The station closed in 1966 but parts of the platform are still in existence.

The box, in Fig. 75, sits opposite a reclaimed building materials site, which was once the goods yard. The finials are more than usually ornate and it still has its locking frame room windows, as one supposes that Beeston was not well known to the Luftwaffe. The Shropshire Union Canal is behind the box on the other side of the hill.

Fig. 76 was taken at the former station site looking towards Chester. The line is canted over on a curve with super-elevation, as the line speed here is 75mph (120km/h).

The ground disc is far back from the trailing crossover and this is probably a sighting issue. The Shropshire Union Canal bridge carrying the A49

road is in the background. The Shropshire Union Canal Company was owned by the LMS.

Fig. 77 shows the remnant of the up side platform towards Crewe with its platform starter signal. A class 67 from DB Schenker intrudes speedily on the scene with a single engineer's coach in tow.

Beeston Castle and Tarporley signal box is 168 miles 60 chains (271.6km) from London Euston station.

The line runs for just over 10 miles (16km) until Chester station is reached. The station is early – from 1848 – and a listed building. It was a creation of Thomas Brassy, the railway contractor who had a major hand in the railways of Britain and elsewhere.

Chester itself is a former Roman garrison town and is steeped in history. It has a complete set of walls around the original city and is famous for the 'Rows' – an early, enclosed sort of shopping mall. Railways from all over Britain advertised Chester as a visitor attraction and so it remains today.

As well as the LMS, Chester was host to the GWR and the LNER at Chester Northgate station. The semaphore signalling scene at Chester station was a busy one, with six signal boxes around the station and two engine sheds and a further one nearby. Apart from the lines to Crewe and

Fig.76   Beeston Castle and
Tarporley looking towards Chester,
December 2014.

Holyhead, Chester has two lines to the Wirral, one
to Manchester and one to Wrexham.

Chester station is 179 miles 11 chains (288.3km)
from Euston.

The line runs along the Roodee by the race-
course, one of the earliest in Britain, before crossing
the River Dee into North Wales.

Mold Junction

Date Built	1902
LNWR Type or Builder	LNWR Type 4+
No. of Levers	30
Ways of Working	AB
Current Status	Demolished 2005
Listed (Y/N)	N

Fig. 77   Beeston Castle and Tarporley looking towards Crewe,
December 2014.

The town of Saltney is the first on our route in North
Wales and part of it is in Cheshire. The national
boundary runs through Boundary Lane.

Saltney expanded as a railway town but had its
origins in boat building along the banks of the River
Dee, part of which was canalized by the Dutch in
the eighteenth century. Saltney had a massive
freight marshalling yard at Mold Junction and the
GWR had a wagon repair factory. Homes were built
by the LNWR for their employees and their families.

Mold Junction is hanging on to life in Fig. 78 with
a few months to go, and it is easy to see where the
tracks all around the box had been. The layout from

Fig. 78   Mold Junction signal box, November 2004.

Fig. 79   Mold Junction looking towards Holyhead, November 2004.

Fig. 80   Sandycroft signal box, November 2004.

just by the city walls in Chester had been quadruple track mostly as far as Llanddulas, the other side of Abergele. The view is towards Chester. The junction in the title was after a line to Mold and Denbigh that closed in the 1960s.

Fig. 79 is the view towards Holyhead, and there is a vestige of mechanical signalling on the right with the de-armed signal post. The former engine shed, coded 6B, still exists as a scrapyard out of shot on the left; it housed ex-LMS and ex-GWR locomotives after the closure of the GWR shed in Chester and its conversion into a DMU depot. The houses on the right are ex-LNWR workers' cottages, and just by them is an ex-LNWR 'barracks', where visiting train crews could stay overnight before setting off back home with another freight train.

Mold Junction was 182 miles 29 chains (293.5km) from Euston.

The line continues along the River Dee estuary past the former RAF Hawarden base, which also housed the De Havilland aircraft factory – which still holds the record for the construction of a Wellington bomber in less than 24 hours during World War II. The factory now makes wings for Airbus and is the major employer in the area.

Sandycroft

Date Built	1900
LNWR Type or Builder	LNWR Type 4+
No. of Levers	60
Ways of Working	AB
Current Status	Demolished 2005
Listed (Y/N)	N

Still following the banks of the River Dee, we reach Sandycroft, which developed as a port to carry coal in pre-main line railway days. There had been tramways and wagonways, some narrow gauge, to transport the coal from collieries at Mancot and Hawarden to vessels at Sandycroft.

In Fig. 80 the box had already been switched out for some years, as declining traffic levels did not need a block post. The capacity of a line with absolute block is one train in each block. The more blocks there are, the denser the traffic pattern can be. Where traffic patterns have increased in AB areas, intermediate block sections, or IBS, have been introduced. This box was on the endangered species list at the time of the photo, with only weeks to go before the end. The tracks nearest to the camera are the up goods loop towards Chester and will go when the box goes. This is one of the last remains of what had been quadruple track.

Sandycroft signal box was 184 miles 73 chains (297.6km) from London Euston.

The line runs from Sandycroft through Queensferry (station closed) and Shotton, which has two stations: the Low Level is the former LNWR coast line and High Level is the former Great Central or LNER line from Wrexham to Bidston in Birkenhead.

Then comes Connah's Quay, which has no station now but did have a wagon repair depot for chlorine tankers until relatively recently. A branch line from the previously described LNER line ran underneath the LNWR to the docks.

The line then runs past a gas-fired power station to Rockcliffe Hall.

Rockcliffe Hall

Date Built	1995
LNWR Type or Builder	BR Portakabin
No. of Levers	IFS panel
Ways of Working	TCB, AB
Current Status	Active
Listed (Y/N)	N

Rockcliffe Hall is almost very aptly named, with just two crossovers to control, but its main function is to act as a 'fringe' box to Chester power box. After

mechanical signalling had been removed at Mold Junction and Sandycroft and the boxes demolished, the track circuit block area was extended this far.

After this it is mostly absolute block and mechanical signalling.

Rockcliffe Hall is 188 miles and 74 chains (304km) from London Euston.

The line then runs past Flint, which has continued the coast tradition of an ancient castle and also has some fine listed station buildings. Flint also had a manufacturing base in textiles with the Courtaulds factory.

Holywell Junction (HJ)

Date Built	1902
LNWR Type or Builder	LNWR Type 4+
No. of Levers	54
Ways of Working	AB
Current Status	Active
Listed (Y/N)	Y

Holywell, as its name suggests, is the site of a holy well, attributed to one St Winifride; it has been known about since Roman times and a pilgrimage site since AD660. Holywell is regarded as the 'Lourdes of Wales'. Naturally this interest generated a branch line from the main line at Greenfield to Holywell, only just over a mile (1.6km) away up a gradient of 1 in 27. Holywell Town station and

Fig. 81 Rockcliffe Hall signal box looking towards Chester, January 2015.

Fig. 82 Holywell Junction signal box, November 2004.

Fig. 83   Holywell Junction looking towards Holyhead, October 2014.

Fig. 84   Holywell Junction signal box and station looking towards Holyhead, October 2014.

Fig. 85   Holywell Junction signal box and station looking towards Chester, October 2014.

the branch line closed to passengers in 1954 and Holywell Junction at Greenfield closed to passengers in 1966.

Greenfield was a major centre for the manufacture of textiles by the Courtaulds company. The station was designed by Francis Thompson, and his individual architectural style is still seen at some places along the route although much of it is now in private hands. The station building and signal box at Holywell Junction are Grade II listed.

Fig. 82 shows how spacious the layout here is, as there used to be an island platform between the two fast lines in quadruple-track days. The layout still echoes those days, as it has up and down goods loops, a further loop on the up side and two further sidings on the down side towards Holyhead. The two running lines are either side of the box. The layout is also on a curve, so most of the signals are bracketed out for sighting reasons.

The Virgin Voyager in Fig. 83 is doing about 75mph (120km/h) at this point on its journey to Chester and Euston. They are among the few diesel-engined trains to be found at Euston. Note the exit ground signals for the up goods loop and the up loop off that. The up goods loop is track circuited, the further loop is not. These signals are only for reversing moves here. The reason for bracketing out the HJ 3 signal is self-evident from this shot. The pampas grass in the front of the box is a retro 1970s touch. The Dee estuary is just visible, as is the 4,450-tonne *Duke of Lancaster*, which was built for British Railways as a passenger ferry and is now beached.

Fig. 84 is still looking towards Holyhead, and here the layout becomes clearer. The down platform with the Francis Thompson station building is on the left. The bracket signal right in front of the camera is HJ 52 and it has a subsidiary red-and-white-striped arm beneath the main arm. The purpose of this arm is to allow a train to pass the HJ 52 at danger for shunting purposes. The up loop extends beyond HJ 52, which is the entry point for the next block section. This is a kind of permissive working where a train is allowed to enter the next block section for a specific purpose.

Note that there had once been another signal on the post or doll at the other end of the bracket – no doubt the section signal for the slow line when it was quadruple track.

Fig. 85 is the opposite view, from the bridge at Dock Road Greenfield, towards Chester. The two fast running lines splay out to admit the island platform, and the two rather rusty goods loops still give an impression of the former grandeur of the tracks here. The down goods loop on the right is actually a headshunt at this point and the crossover with power-operated points is just starting at the bottom right of the picture. The subsidiary arm on the bracket controls entry to the down goods loop. Similarly, on the up side, on the left the track beyond the crossover is a headshunt. The crossover points are also power operated. The two track-circuited ground discs signal either straight on up the headshunt or out onto the up main line. The A548 road that runs parallel with the main line at Greenfield still has the imposing brick bridge over it to carry the Holywell branch line.

Holywell Junction signal box is 195 miles 76 chains (315.4km) from London Euston.

Mostyn (MN)

Date Built	1902
LNWR Type or Builder	LNWR Type 4
No. of Levers	40
Ways of Working	AB
Current Status	Active (switched out)
Listed (Y/N)	Y

The port of Mostyn takes its name from the village nearby and in turn from the Mostyn family, who were awarded lands from a grateful King Henry VII. The family has substantial property and interests in the area and in Llandudno, up the coast, there is the Mostyn Art Gallery. The port developed from the need to export the steel manufactured there, supported by local collieries.

The port now supports offshore wind farms and the export of the larger Airbus wings that have been carried by barge down the River Dee

Fig. 86   Mostyn signal box, October 2014.

Fig. 87   Mostyn signal box looking towards Holyhead, October 2014.

from the factory at Broughton near the site of Mold Junction. The smaller aircraft wings are flown out of Broughton in Beluga aircraft.

Mostyn signal box in Fig. 86 has something of the look of Severn Bridge Junction at Shrewsbury, with the double-decker locking frame room. It might have suffered the same fate as Mold Junction or Sandycroft had it not been listed, and some of the infrastructure of the port remains. The box has been switched out for some years now but retains the link to the port, where steel had been loaded until the local steelworks closed in 1965.

Like Holywell Junction, Mostyn signal box is also sandwiched between the two main running lines, but the clearances dictated a narrow box with an overhanging operating floor. The view in Fig. 87 is towards Holyhead, and the left-hand point is part

Fig. 88 Mostyn signal box yard and dock lines, October 2014.

Fig. 89 Mostyn approaches from Chester, October 2014.

of a crossover between the two running lines. The right-hand point, leading to a loop and sidings, has four detection slides on its left for four ground discs. The goods shed and another Francis Thompson station building, both in private hands, are in the distance on the down side on the left; both these buildings are better viewed from the A548.

Both home signals are off in Fig. 88 (looking towards Holyhead) as the box is switched out.

The reason for the detection slides on the entry point to the dock sidings now becomes clear, with all four ground discs in view. The box rear wall is just on the left.

In the other direction but still looking towards Holywell, Fig. 89 shows more home signals pulled off. One of these is on a gantry, which is odd as it is on its own, but perhaps there were once others to accompany it. The dock offices and light industrial buildings make up the scene. The far track is a continuation of the headshunt we saw in Fig. 88.

Mostyn signal box is 199 miles 12 chains (320.5km) from London Euston.

Talacre (TE)

Date Built	1903
LNWR Type or Builder	LNWR Type 4
No. of Levers	24
Ways of Working	AB
Current Status	Active
Listed (Y/N)	N

Talacre is just by the Point of Ayr, which is where the River Dee meets the Irish Sea and the first of the North Wales holiday resorts is encountered. It was also the place where the last deep-mined coal in North Wales was excavated at Point of Ayr colliery, which closed in 1996. The track infrastructure that supported the colliery largely still remains. The coal trains later supplied Fiddlers Ferry power station, which we shall encounter again on the Widnes–Warrington section. Natural gas is now brought ashore at Point of Ayr, so the energy connection remains.

Fig. 90 Talacre signal box, October 2014.

Talacre signal box (Fig. 90) was originally at Gronant, which is a village just up the coast nearer Prestatyn. The light industrial unit behind occupies some of the site of the colliery but behind that are Talacre beach holiday homes.

In Fig. 91, the bridge by the second crossover is the Station Road bridge and leads to Talacre beach. The double-track main line is to the left and splays out after the bridge to accommodate an island platform. This, together with the remains of the platform on view past the bridge and one the other side of the down main line, gave a station with four platforms in all – typical of many of the stations on the line as far as Abergele. The station closed in 1966.

The rusty track on the right is the remains of the Point of Ayr colliery loop and headshunt and, by the box, a siding leading off to the colliery yard.

Fig. 92 is the view back towards Mostyn docks, which can be seen in the distance. The double siding entry into the colliery is where double-headed class 20s assembled the merry-go-round hopper wagon trains before setting off for Fidlers Ferry towards Chester and Warrington. The yellow box between the tracks on the down main line is an AWS ramp. AWS (automatic warning system) can sense when a train has passed a signal and gives warnings or, in exceptional cases, can apply the brakes if a train has run past a signal at danger. It is a kind of vigilance prompter that alerts drivers to the presence of a signal and its aspect. The small posts between the tracks are to aid the tracked to be canted over at the correct angle of super-elevation to enable trains to

Fig. 91   *Talacre looking towards Holyhead, October 2014.*

take curves at higher speeds. A Pendolino train enhances this feature by leaning into the curve much as a motorcyclist might do on a bend.

Talacre signal box is 201 miles 76 chains (325km) from Euston.

Prestatyn (PN)

Date Built	*c.*1897
LNWR Type or Builder	LNWR Type 4
No. of Levers	45
Ways of Working	AB
Current Status	Active
Listed (Y/N)	N

Prestatyn is 'round the corner' on the north Wales coast and the first seaside holiday resort on the journey that just looks out over the Irish Sea. Prestatyn's history goes back to Roman times and it is the northern end of Offa's Dyke Path, but the

Fig. 92   *Talacre looking towards Chester, November 2004.*

Fig. 93   Prestatyn signal box, October 2014.

Fig. 94   Prestatyn station looking towards Chester, January 2005.

Fig. 95   Prestatyn station island platform looking towards Chester, January 2005.

village of 1,000 grew in the nineteenth century to almost twenty times that size with the coming of the railway. Later on, holiday camps sprung up and these were used by the military in World War II. Many thousands of children were sent to Prestatyn to escape the bombing of Liverpool and Manchester. The only bomb damage suffered at Prestatyn was, bizarrely, at the hands of the Italian Air Force.

Prestatyn signal box, in Fig. 93, looks almost lost in the vegetation, but this is simply the result of reducing the running lines to double from quadruple track.

The box was extended in 1931 from thirty-one levers to the present forty-five, and the extension to the windows and brickwork can be clearly seen on the left-hand side.

Fig. 94 shows the down platform at Prestatyn station looking towards Talacre and Chester. There is a glimpse of the old goods shed on the right. This exists next to the original brick-built station building, which now sees a new use.

In the distance are a bracketed-out and a home signal on a gantry, the latter a remnant of the quadruple-track era.

Fig. 95, looking towards Chester, gives a view of the fine LNWR wooden station building and canopy. The other two platforms, now track-less, can be seen, together with some creative gardening.

Distant signals in the wild are quite rare. In Fig. 96 Prestatyn's up distant is giving the nod to a class 175 Coradia, 175 003, on its way to Chester and Manchester Piccadilly. Rhyl is the town in the background and it is Rhyl's down colour light distant signal. A single-track branch line to Dyserth left the main line from here, and this stretch of track had water troughs to replenish steam engines on the move.

Inside the box, the block shelf in Fig. 97 shows the BR standard 'domino' absolute block instruments. The one on the left is for the lines towards Rhyl and the one on the right towards Talacre.

If a train is going towards Rhyl, that box has to signal first Line Clear and then Train on Line. If it is coming from Rhyl, Prestatyn has to give

Line Clear followed by Train on Line when appropriate.

If a train is on the up line to Talacre (that is, towards Euston) then it is up to Talacre to signal it; conversely, if it is coming from Talacre on the down line, Prestatyn has to signal it.

The wooden box with the brass switch on the front is the block switch, and its current state is open. Come night time, when no passenger trains are running, the off-going signaller pulls off all signals and sets the block switch state to 'closed'. This then means that Rhyl and Talacre pass trains along the route. The object sitting on top of the block switch is a Bardic lamp, which can display three colours and is used for hand signals at night if all else has failed. Flags are also issued as standard but for daytime emergencies.

There also used to be megaphones but they are not so evident any more. They were a kind of asynchronous broadband connection in that the download data speed from the signaller always comfortably exceeded the upload speed from the train driver.

The circular objects with the winding handle are a Welwyn Release. These came into use after an accident in 1935 on the LNER when a train was accepted into a section that was already occupied. As a consequence, points and signals were further interlocked with track circuits and block instruments. This can lead to a gridlock if a track circuit fails as they are always fail-safe and no signals could be pulled off. The release introduces a timer, at the end of which the Welwyn Control can be overridden.

The circular instruments on the front of the block shelf show signal status or position. The lit instrument is showing the status of a power supply but these types can be used to show signal status.

On the far right is the edge of the diagram and we can see that the up distant is 1,902yd (1,739m) from the home signal and is shown bracketed out, which is accurate as we have seen in Fig. 96. The distant signal coming from Talacre is a colour light.

Fig. 98 is the lever frame at Prestatyn signal box and it is pointless. There is no black point or blue

Fig. 96   Prestatyn signal box's distant signal looking towards Rhyl, January 2015.

Fig. 97   Prestatyn signal box block instrument shelf, October 2014.

facing-point lock levers. Some of the disused white levers have had the 'ring pull' or stirrup handle removed. We can see from here that the yellow distant signal lever, further away towards the Rhyl end, is normal size, indicating it is a semaphore, and the one nearest the camera is cut down and is the colour light switch lever.

There are more signal status indicators screwed to the front of the block shelf, and the large black box at the far end of the block shelf is a 'lamp out' indicator for signals that cannot be seen from the box. A buzzer will ring and a light will illuminate if the light has failed and there is a switch to test the circuit on the unit. At night or in low light conditions, a lamp out on a semaphore signal is the same

Fig. 98   Prestatyn signal box lever frame, October 2014.

Fig. 99   Prestatyn signal box signal wire adjusters, October 2014.

as a failed signal or one that cannot be seen. These circuits usually work on monitoring the current flow in the circuit and a failed lamp or broken circuit results in no current flow.

Notice on the diagram how far the box is from the running line, indicating that there were more running lines originally. Note also how worn and polished the piece of wood is in front of the levers. Generations of signallers have used this wood to gain purchase to pull over the levers.

Fig. 99 shows a detail of the lever frame. Here the semaphore distant lever, No. 14, is of interest, the same signal as in Fig. 96. The same number 14 appears on the signal plate as on the diagram, and the ivorine plate beneath the handle declares that the two home signals 15 and 17, which are nearby in the frame, need to be pulled first. The mechanical

locking in the frame room downstairs needs this to happen before it will allow No. 14 to be pulled off. Note that signal 17 has a white stripe on the lever body and this is to indicate that there is an electrical lock on the lever as well as a mechanical one. The gadget by the wall underneath the window is the screw adjuster for signal 14 that is needed to take up the expansion of the well over a mile (1.6km) of signal wire in hot weather.

Prestatyn signal box is 205 miles 43 chains (330.8km) from London Euston; and the station, measured from the centre of the platform, is 9 chains (180m) less.

Rhyl (RL)

Date Built	1900
LNWR Type or Builder	LNWR Type 4
No. of Levers	90
Ways of Working	AB
Current Status	Active
Listed (Y/N)	Y

The fact that the railway was quadruple track from Chester to just beyond Abergele is largely a measure of the popularity of Rhyl as a holiday resort. The station was built on an expansive scale to cope with hundreds of holidaymakers arriving at once, and excursion trains queuing to occupy a platform. The broad platforms and commodious footbridge still

Fig. 100　Rhyl signal box, January 2015.

Fig. 101　East end of Rhyl station and signal box, January 2015.

bear witness to the unrelenting throngs of people there were here. The station buildings are extraordinarily large compared with any other station on the line bar Chester and Crewe.

In common with many other British holiday resorts, Rhyl suffered a decline but is bravely fighting back and trying to win its share of 'staycationers'.

To support this entire railway activity there are two LNWR signal boxes, Rhyl No. 1 and Rhyl No. 2. Both are listed buildings but only Rhyl No. 1 is operational and now simply plated as Rhyl, although the box retains its original title on the end (Fig. 100). If the name plate were changed that might contravene the rules about Grade II listing and may require special permission.

The reinforcement to the walkway with the vertical stanchions seems to be a local thing as Rhyl No. 2 has this too.

The class 175 Coradia – 175 116 – sets out for the up Chester direction in Fig. 101, and the destination given on the scrolling caption is Maesteg, which is a small station in South Wales near Bridgend. This is about 120 miles (200km) away.

The east end of Rhyl station can be seen from the Grange Road bridge with two facing points – one for the crossover and one for the passenger loop line. The bridge gives an indication of how many tracks there were here. To the left was the goods yard and a further platform, making the current left-hand platform an island. There were a number of carriage sidings here – reduced to two now – for use by engineer's trains. The massive footbridge is just visible and there is a hint of the extent of the station buildings on the up, right-hand side.

The grandeur may be slightly faded, but Rhyl station is still impressive, seen from platform 2 in Fig. 102. A further platform ran round the back of the current platform 2 to make an island, and the goods yard was behind that.

There was a branch line to Denbigh that closed in the 1950s, and the bay platforms were behind the camera and between the island platforms. There was also a single-track branch line to Dyserth towards Prestatyn that was serviced from Rhyl.

Fig. 102　Rhyl station looking towards Chester, January 2015.

Fig. 103   Rhyl station looking towards Holyhead, January 2015.

In addition there was also a locomotive turntable here, as well as a steam loco depot coded 6K. Morrison's supermarket now occupies much of what had been railway real estate.

The track on the near platform is wooden sleepers with keyed chair track with bullhead rail, so this could have seen some of 6K's residents. This is almost as it must have looked but for one road missing near platform 1 on the far side. The signalling has been much simplified and the starter at platform 1 is off. The platforms are still their original length, which is unusual, and there are staff here.

Fig. 103 is the view towards Abergele and Holyhead, with the track snaking round and heading back to the coast line. Rhyl No. 2 is at the end of platform 1, and if there was an ivy league for signal boxes, this one would be a contender. Rhyl No. 2 was even larger, lever count-wise, than Rhyl No. 1, with 126 levers. Signal RL 101 is to enable platform 1 to be bi-directional, and the facing crossover seen in Fig. 101 gives access to the platform from the down running line. The other two semaphores are for the platform 2 starter on the left and the through down running line. There are red colour lights further up the line for both. The down passenger loop extends for well over half a mile (1km) in total.

In Fig. 104 Rhyl No. 2 signal box is an imposing if somewhat eerie sight, with all the windows boarded up. The front wall has started to bulge out at some point judging by all the circular discs in two rows to hold it in. This box would appear to be internally staircased as with No. 1, although No. 1

Fig. 104   Rhyl No. 2 signal box, January 2015.

does have a fire escape ladder on the outside. Note also that there is an additional 'doll' or post on the signal bracket.

Both Rhyl and Prestatyn had LMS Patriot class 4–6–0 express passenger locomotives named after them. Other resorts along the coast were also so honoured.

Rhyl station is 209 miles and 8 chains (336.5km) from London Euston.

Abergele (AE)

Date Built	1900
LNWR Type or Builder	LNWR Type 4
No. of Levers	60
Ways of Working	AB
Current Status	Active
Listed (Y/N)	Y

Abergele is an attractive small market town that is often overshadowed as a holiday resort by its larger neighbours of Rhyl and Colwyn Bay. It forms part of the almost continuous resort presence from Prestatyn, Rhyl, Towyn, Pensarn and Abergele. There is a large static caravan presence from Towyn onwards.

In 1868 there was an accident at Abergele that was to have far-reaching effects on railway practices generally. A pickup goods train was making its way from Crewe to Holyhead, shunting goods yards and picking up and setting down wagons as required. It became necessary to leave some wagons on the main line whilst part of the shunting was carried out. A rough shunt by the locomotive caused the wagons to recoil and begin to run down the gradient towards Abergele station.

The Irish Mail had left Chester four minutes late and was working hard to recover the lost time when it came upon the runaways and was derailed. Wagons full of paraffin casks together with gas lighting cylinders in the coaches was a recipe for disaster and in the ensuing fire thirty-three people lost their lives. The memorial to the dead is still there in Abergele church graveyard. After that there was a change in the way goods wagons were handled and headshunts, which we have seen already in this book, became commonplace. A headshunt enables a yard to be shunted clear of the main running lines. They are sometimes called a 'shunting neck'.

Abergele and Pensarn signal box, as its name plate says, is yet another listed LNWR box on this route (Fig. 105). This had also been an island platform station but unlike Prestatyn, where the island survives, at Abergele the flanking platforms remain. Platform 1 at the far side abuts the sea defences and then there is the beach. Station buildings have survived on both remaining platforms. The signal to the right of the box is a banner repeater, and we shall see this in action later.

Fig. 106 is the view down platform 2. The layout here consists of a single loop on the down side, and

Fig. 105   Abergele signal box, January 2015.

Fig. 106   Abergele station looking towards Holyhead, January 2015.

Fig. 107   Abergele station looking towards Chester, January 2015.

we are looking towards Llandudno Junction and Holyhead. The signal on the left is the platform 2 starter, the next one is the down main line – and this is the signal for which there is a banner repeater opposite the end of platform 2. Moving across the track to the up main, the signal here has a sighting board and is off for a train. The traffic lights can't help, particularly when they are red and it's night.

Fig. 107 is the view from the overbridge in Fig. 106 looking towards Chester and Crewe. Note how there is only one rod coming from the box for the down loop point whereas the carrier can accommodate a maximum of eight. Platform 1 on the left and its starter signal can just be seen beyond the footbridge to the beach. Almost opposite the starter are two posts held together and these are

the down main and platform 2 loop line signals. The taller signal for the down main is hidden by the footbridge.

Fig. 108 is looking the other way, from the Tennis Court Road footbridge. The banner repeater, AE 3 BR, for the down main, is telling us the signal is on. It must be because the point for the down loop is set for the loop, and the banner repeater is for the down main. Note also that the signal for the platform 2 loop is still on at this point, and it could be that the train may be held here.

Note the quarter-mile post, painted yellow, is on the down side on the left.

The class 175 Coradia in platform 1 is 175 111.

In Fig. 109 the class 175 Coradia 175 089 accelerates towards Chester from platform 1, which we saw in Fig. 108 looking the other way from the Tennis Court Road footbridge. The platform 1 starter is on the left. Note the backlight blinder that looks a bit like a herb chopper on the rear of the arm – this will move up, obscuring the backlight, when the signal is pulled off.

Fig. 108   Abergele station looking west to Holyhead, January 2015.

In Fig. 110 the down main signal is off for the class 175 Coradia 175 118, which is bypassing platform 2 as it is not stopping at Abergele on this trip. The lower arm is for platform 2, and the LNWR often arranged their signals like this, although this is an LMS/LMR replacement. A bracket signal might be more elegant but is more costly, as the bracketed arm has to be cantilevered out and that takes a larger post and massive foundations to support it. The metal grid between the rails near the signal posts is a train protection and warning system (TPWS) transducer, which conveys the signal aspect to the train and will stop it if the signal has been passed at danger.

Fig. 109 Abergele station approaches looking east to Chester, January 2015.

The same train, 175 118, is shown again in Fig. 111 but the view is expanded to show the aspect of the banner repeater being off. The traffic lights have turned red.

In Fig. 112 a DB Schenker class 67, 67 027, pushes four Network Rail coaches with a driving trailer at the front towards Llandudno Junction.

You don't find a class 67 pushing coaches very often and then two show up within minutes of each other. Class 67, 67 001 in Arriva livery in Fig. 113, is pushing five Arriva-liveried coaches with driving trailer, from platform 1 headed for Chester.

Class 175 Coradia 175 108 calls in at platform 2 on its way to Llandudno in Fig. 114; note the signal the other side of the footbridge is still off.

In Fig. 115 Coradia 175 108 now has the 'road' from the starter, and the guard or conductor is back in the trailer car as the unit departs for Llandudno.

In Fig. 116 a ten-car Virgin Voyager, first stop Chester, hurtles past signal AE 59 past platform 1

Fig. 110 Abergele station approaches with a class 175 arriving from Chester, January 2015.

Fig. 111 Class 175 signalled to avoid stopping at Abergele station, January 2015.

Fig. 112   Abergele station with a class 67 pushing a Network Rail train towards Holyhead, January 2015.

Fig. 113   Abergele station with a class 67 pushing an Arriva train towards Chester, January 2015.

Fig. 114   Class 175 signalled into the platform at Abergele station, January 2015.

Fig. 115   Class 175 signalled for departure to Llandudno at Abergele station, January 2015.

Fig. 116   Abergele station with a Virgin Voyager racing for Chester from Holyhead, January 2015.

Fig. 117   Abergele station and overbridge, January 2015.

and the coast line. Happily the traffic lights have no say in the matter.

Fig. 117 shows signal AE 59 close up. Note the yellow disc-shaped object to the right of the signal arm. This is a signal arm transducer and relays the position of the arm to the signaller, as this signal is not visible from the box. For the same reason, no hole has been cut in the sighting board to display a backlight. The station building up on the roadway is a delight and well restored but not in use. The roadway of the actual bridge is cobbled to add to the period feel.

Abergele and Pensarn station is 213 miles and 30 chains (343.4km) from London Euston.

The line continues past Colwyn Bay, which was another popular holiday resort with a station to match, but the layout suffered when the A55 Expressway was built.

Then the line arrives at the only true junction left – Llandudno Junction.

Llandudno Junction (LJ)

Date Built	1985
LNWR Type or Builder	BR LMR Type 15c
No. of Levers	Nx panel
Ways of Working	AB
Current Status	Active
Listed (Y/N)	Y

Llandudno Junction was such a railway conurbation that they named a town after it. It had a large station, which mostly survives; and signal boxes, goods yard, engine shed and carriage sidings and shed, which have not. There is a street in Llandudno Junction called Ffordd 6G Road (*ffordd* being road in Welsh) to commemorate the locomotive depot coded 6G. After the steam depot closed in 1966 diesels were housed in the old carriage sheds.

Fig. 118 shows a box that was the replacement for a Rhyl signal box-type LNWR structure; At the same time, all the mechanical signalling was jettisoned in favour of colour lights.

The lever frame was also replaced by an Nx panel. This is so called because it has a track layout representation with an eNtrance and eXit on it as the tracks pass through its area. The panels are usually made of an aluminium frame into which are inserted plastic tiles, which may have part of a

Fig. 118   Llandudno Junction signal box, January 2015.

Fig. 119   Llandudno Junction west of
the station, January 2015.

track represented on them or hold a light or switch. This means it is relatively simple matter to make changes.

The principle of operation is that a single switch at the entrance to a route is set together with another single switch at the exit point. The relay interlocking then figures out which points and signals need to be selected to achieve the desired route. Points and signals have their own discrete switches but they are normally left in automatic mode to operate as described. Should an extraordinary move be required, the requisite switches are selected to manual by the signaller, then individually operated. The box controls access to the two branches to

Fig. 120   Llandudno Junction station, west end, January 2015.

Llandudno and Blaenau Ffestiniog, working AB to the former and key token to the latter.

Llandudno Junction appears again in Fig. 119, which shows some of the junctions. From the left, the first is the 'Quay Siding', which has a run-round loop and loco release crossover. Next to that is the down main (on the left) and up main to/from Bangor and Holyhead curving round to the left to line up to cross the River Conway, and beyond is part of Conway town in the distance. The last two lines are the branch to Llandudno, and the down main point to the terminus is set for that. There are other crossovers that allow access to/from the running lies and platforms at the junction station.

Llandudno Junction station is viewed from Ffordd 6G Road in Fig. 120, looking towards Chester.

On the far left is the tamper siding, where track-maintenance vehicles are stabled, and to the right of that is a non-electronic banner repeater signal that is off for the adjacent platform. Many of the Blaenau Ffestiniog trains call here on their way to Llandudno.

The banner repeater refers to station platform 1, and this also has the Network Rail staff mess room. This contains the ancillary token apparatus for the Blaenau Ffestiniog branch, which means that train drivers need only go the mess room to withdraw or surrender a token rather than trek over running

Fig. 121   Class 175 leaving from Llandudno Junction station, January 2015.

lines to the signal box. There is also a ticket office between platforms here.

Platform 2 is the bay platform for branch trains to Llandudno, which is used to operate a shuttle service to the town. There are other trains from Llandudno that go beyond the junction, as we saw at Abergele, and they use the through platforms. The other bay has no track and is disused but both have steam age buffer stops. The buffer stops look capable of securing the RMS *Queen Mary* at the very least and this is probably why they have survived.

Platform 3 is the major platform for express arrivals and departures and has a buffet and waiting room on the island.

Finally, on the right is platform 4, which is sometimes used by the Blaenau Ffestiniog branch trains.

The birch trees on the far right hide a series of loops and beyond that is a disused oil and coal depot.

Still looking towards Chester, a class 175 Coradia, 175 115, headed for Bangor, is waiting for the off at platform 3 in Fig. 121. The formidable buffer stops are in view and there are notices advising trains not to contact the stops – sensible advice given that most trains no longer have buffers as such and only a front coupling unit. The footbridge is after the style of the Rhyl example and capable of handling throngs of people.

In Fig. 122 the class 175 departs past LJ 65, which has a theatre-type route indicator and is showing M

Fig. 122   Class 175 departing from Llandudno Junction station past a theatre-style route indicator, January 2015.

for main, or the line to Bangor and Holyhead. The train is on the up side at the moment and must cross over to the down side to continue its journey. The other option would be L for Llandudno.

A class 158, 158 828, two-car DMU sets off for Deganwy and Llandudno on the shuttle service in Fig. 123. Deganwy has been demoted to a request stop.

Turning to the other end of the station now, looking towards Chester, a Virgin Trains Voyager unit on the down main is drawing near to platform 3 in Fig. 124. Roughly where the last vehicle

Fig. 123   Llandudno Junction station with a class 158 departing for Llandudno, January 2015.

Fig. 124   Llandudno Junction station east end, January 2015.

in the train is, the Blaenau Ffestiniog branch up the Conway valley veers off to the right. Signal LJ 64, straight in front of the camera, has a 'feather' or branch indicator for the Conway valley. LJ 62, on the left, has two feathers, one for the crossover to the up main, and the 90-degree one for the Conway valley. Note that there is a Virgin Trains stop board (VT Stop) on the lamp post on the far left and that is a ten-coach pull-up point. The disused freight facilities are a little more visible here on the far right. Snowdonia, in the distance, looks as though it might be chilly.

Just by signal LJ 62 is the ground frame in Fig. 125. It controls access to the tamper siding of which we saw the end in Fig. 120. The blue/brown lever is provided with an electrical lock from the box,

and when this is released by the signaller in the box, the frame can be used by another operator. The siding has a trap point that co-acts with the point that lets the tamper siding out onto the platform 1 line. One lever moves both point and trap point but not before the facing-point lock lever (in blue) has been unlocked first. After the point has been changed over, the facing-point lock lever is set back to normal as shown to re-lock the point in the new position. The red lever is for a ground signal to enable a train to reverse into the siding. Any other train movements have to be signalled with hand signals by the person who is operating the ground frame.

Llandudno Junction station is 223 miles 39 chains (359.7km) from London Euston.

Fig. 125   Llandudno Junction station ground frame, January 2015.

Fig. 126   Deganwy signal box, January 2015.

Llandudno Branch

This double-track line takes us to Deganwy on the beautiful River Conway estuary and then to charming Llandudno with the Great Orme as a backdrop. This journey is only just over 3 miles (5km) from Llandudno Junction and the mileages, hitherto calculated from Euston, are from Llandudno Junction station.

Deganwy (DY)

Date Built	1914
LNWR Type or Builder	LNWR Type 5+
No. of Levers	18
Ways of Working	AB
Current Status	Active
Listed (Y/N)	N

Deganwy is a pretty village on the banks of the Conway estuary and once had an ancient castle that succumbed after Edward I built Conway Castle. The LNWR built a quay to enable the export

of roofing slates from quarries around Blaenau Ffestiniog. This is now a marina for pleasure craft but the road access to it is a crossing controlled by the signal box.

Deganwy signal box has only signals and two crossings to control (Fig. 126). There is also a green bell just by the drainpipe to ring to advise passengers that a train is due, although this requirement has largely been overtaken by the provision of moving message displays that update in real time. The signal box is unusual in that it has a stone base.

Fig. 127 was taken from the original footbridge looking towards Llandudno Junction station, and the view is all colour lights. The Quay crossing is visible and the River Conway is right next door. It is tidal at this point.

Fig. 127   Deganwy looking towards Llandudno Junction, January 2015.

Fig. 128   Deganwy station looking towards Llandudno station, January 2015.

Looking towards Llandudno from Deganwy station in Fig. 128, a view of the estuary and the sea is thrown in.

Fig. 129 shows how the lines curve sharply to Llandudno; both curves are check railed to emphasize this.

A short way out of Deganwy towards Llandudno, Fig. 130 shows the end of the check-railed curve seen in Fig. 129, and signal DY 6 on the up side. Further towards Llandudno is Deganwy's motor-operated distant signal, but this is not in shot.

On the down side, the distant, which would be Llandudno's, is a fixed board. Some 1,300yd (1,190m) on and after the fixed distant is Llandudno's outer home signal. Fixed distants are usually placed where the line speed is 40mph (64km/h) or less. The Great Orme is in the background.

Deganwy station is 1 mile 16 chains (1.9km) from Llandudno Junction station.

Llandudno (LO)

Date Built	1891
LNWR Type or Builder	LNWR Type 4+
No. of Levers	34
Ways of Working	AB
Current Status	Active
Listed (Y/N)	N

Llandudno acquired the title of 'Queen of Resorts' as early as 1864, after the railway had arrived. It sits on a sweeping bay and boasts a promenade enclosed between the Great and Little Orme headlands. The pier, which is still intact, was also a ferry terminal for boats to Liverpool and elsewhere.

There are many fine buildings in Llandudno, including some examples in the art nouveau style of the 1890s.

The Great Orme was a centre for mining copper in early times and then developed into a tourist attraction, with the Great Orme Tramway to take

Fig. 129   Deganwy signal box and line curving to Llandudno station, January 2015.

Fig. 130   Deganwy home signal and line to Llandudno station, January 2015.

Fig. 131   Llandudno outer home signal, January 2015.

Fig. 132   Llandudno station approach and carriage sidings,
January 2015.

visitors to the top. The tramway has been faithfully restored but has operated as a cable-hauled system after the overhead catenary was taken down years ago. There is also an overhead cable car system to ascend the summit.

In steam days passengers with business in Manchester were conveyed there in special express trains.

In Fig. 131 we are still on the way from Deganwy at Llandudno Maesdu Golf Course. The view from the Maesdu Road overbridge is of Llandudno's outer home, LO 9, on the up side towards Deganwy. The down side signal has a conventional home signal with a red-and-white-striped subsidiary arm, signals 33 and 34. These usually have a calling on function, where a platform may already be occupied by a train but another is to join it under strict caution. There is also a route indicator to signify which platform the train is headed for. Snowdonia still looks cold.

Llandudno station's approach is the other side view from the Maesdu Road bridge (Fig. 132). The down sidings on the left have been recently pared down to two from three. The up sidings and ground frame (not in shot) on the right appeared disused, particularly when there is a signalling cabinet in the 'four foot' between the tracks. Signals LO 32 and 31 are similar to the previous 33 and 34, and enable a signaller to stack a train at both signals.

Fig. 133 shows Llandudno signal box, just at the station throat. The six locking frame windows have been bricked up. The box was formerly Llandudno No. 2, with more levers, but it has survived, like so many other seaside resorts' signal boxes.

Fig. 134 shows Llandudno station platform ends and their signals. From left to right, the platforms are numbers 1, 2 and 3. Platforms 2 and 3 are extraordinarily wide and there is a roadway between then that would admit vehicles – it must have seen hansom cabs as well as motorized types. The roadway is still paved with granite blocks called 'setts'. The subsidiary armed signals admit

Fig. 133   Llandudno station signal box, January 2015.

Fig. 134   Llandudno station platform signals, January 2015.

Fig. 135   Llandudno station, January 2015.

trains to the down carriage sidings we saw in Fig. 132. Semaphore-signalled gantries are quite rare now, and the old LNWR trick of networking two signals together so that the one supports the other is plain to see on the right. The start of the carriage sidings is by the ground disc signal past the box.

Finally at Llandudno station we reach the same type of buffer stops (Fig. 135) as at Llandudno Junction. The overall roof used to extend as far as the brick supporting wall on the left. The roadway between platforms 2 and 3 is in view. All the platforms were gated off to keep the thronging crowds safe until it was time to board their trains, and the gate posts have the intertwined letters of the LMSR Company adorning them.

Llandudno station is 3 miles 14 chains (5.1km) from Llandudno Junction station.

Blaenau Ffestiniog Branch

This single-track line runs through the beautiful Conway valley to Blaenau Ffestiniog, which was a centre for the slate industry in North Wales. Not only was the Ffestiniog Railway created to take the slate to market by sea at Portmadoc, but the Great Western got in on the act at Minffordd with their exchange sidings as well as their branch line from the town to Bala and ultimately Ruabon. The LNWR, not to be outdone, took slate from Blaenau down this branch to Deganwy for shipment. There were other ports built along the coast to take the slate from Penrhyn and Dinorwic quarries. The branch still sees occasional freight trains in the shape of DRS nuclear flask trains in the wake of the decommissioning of Trawsfynydd nuclear power station.

Glan Conway Station

This is an unscheduled stop on the line and an early one but it is useful to see the lie of the land.

Fig. 136 is looking back from the platform at Glan Conway station towards Llandudno Junction. On the extreme left is Robert Stephenson's tubular bridge over the River Conway taking the North Wales Coast Line to Conway and beyond. Just to the right of the bridge and beyond it is Deganwy and just to the right of that is Llandudno Junction and station. The Great Orme is the larger hill, still further on the right.

The distant colour light signal up the track is Llandudno Junction's LJ 59 R, which is a repeater for LJ 59, further towards the junction. Just visible on the extreme right is the LNWR station building, now in private hands.

Glan Conway station is 1 mile 39 chains (2.4km) from Llandudno Junction.

Llanrwst North (LT)

Date Built	1880
LNWR Type or Builder	LNWR Type 4+
No. of Levers	20
Ways of Working	KT, NSKT
Current Status	Active
Listed (Y/N)	N

Llanrwst is an attractive small town on the River Conway that developed as a result of the wool trade and then diversified into clock and harp making. As it lies near the Snowdonia National Park its main activity today is tourism.

Llanrwst is blessed with two stations but we are only concerned with Llanrwst North, as it has all the signalling locally.

Fig. 137 is a through-the-keyhole view of Llanrwst North station and signal box. The layout here is simply a passing loop, which is train operated; there are only four working levers.

The box works key token with Llandudno Junction and no signaller key token from the box to Blaenau Ffestiniog and beyond to the former nuclear power station at Trawsfynydd.

The key token system requires apparatus at both ends of a section. The section we are concerned with is from Llandudno Junction to Llanrwst, or LJ to LT, to use their abbreviations. Before the driver can withdraw a token from the machine on platform 1 at LJ, there must not have been a token issued at LT. After the token has been removed from LJ, no token can be issued at LT.

The driver, who has now been issued with the authority to proceed, can set off for LT but must still obey any lineside signals or commands issued by a signaller over the GSM-R mobile phone system.

Fig. 136   Glan Conway station, January 2015.

Fig. 137   Llanrwst station approach, January 2015.

Fig. 138   Llanrwst station, January 2015.

Fig. 139   Llanrwst signal box key token exchange, January 2015.

Upon arrival at LT, the driver must surrender the token, which is then inserted into the machine to free up the line for trains in either direction from LJ to LT.

With no signaller key token there is only one token apparatus at LT. A token is issued as before and usually no further tokens can be issued, although certain sections can allow a further token to be issued. There is an example at Kirkby, on Merseyside, where a train travels down the line and then is locked into a siding or loop, allowing another token to be issued for a train to proceed.

The more usual system, however, is for the token to be a physical key that operates ground frames along the route, and this is done by the train driver. The token is then returned to the start point, whence a further token can be issued.

All this means that at Llanrwst drivers coming from Blaenau Ffestiniog must surrender the token for that section and pick up a different one for the journey to Llandudno Junction. Conversely, as we shall see below, the driver coming from Llandudno Junction must surrender that token and pick up a different one for Blaenau Ffestiniog. It is the driver's responsibility to ensure the correct token has been received for the section to be travelled on.

In Fig. 138 a class 150, 150 227, has arrived at Llanrwst station from Llandudno Junction. The class 150 clearly shows a lamp bracket to the left of the corridor connection, which is a relic of an earlier time. Note that there are wheelchair access ramps on both platforms. The loop points are automatically operated by trains. At Llanrwst none of the signals are plated with the lozenge to indicate they are track circuited which is unusual on passenger carrying lines.

Also note that there are original station buildings on both sides of the loop. The double-track goods shed here has found a different use.

Fig. 139 was taken in an attempt to catch them at it, so to speak. The signaller waits by the box, token for Blaenau in the hoop pouch ready to swap with the Llandudno Junction token. When the signaller has received the token surrendered by the driver it is placed in the red Tyer's instrument that can be seen through the box window, once it has been removed from the hoop pouch. This would enable a further train to leave Llandudno Junction or, more likely, a train from Blaenau Ffestiniog to proceed to Llandudno Junction. The driver then proceeds with the Blaenau token, which was withdrawn from a separate instrument. Unfortunately the actual change-over was masked by the disobliging class 150 trailer car.

Note the stack of timber sleepers; there were also rails and builder's bags full of rail chair keys or wooden blocks for the bullhead track.

Fig. 140 shows Llanrwst signal box again, and the track on the right leads to Blaenau Ffestiniog. At the nearer end of the box, through the window, is the red Blaenau token apparatus for the NSKT working. The goods yard starts where the industrial unit is, and the old goods shed is behind the station building.

Llanrwst North station is 11 miles 17 chains (18km) from Llandudno Junction.

Blaenau Ffestiniog Station

In Fig. 141 a class 153, 153 323, is waiting at Blaenau Ffestiniog station in earlier years. At both ends of the loop are ground frames where the train driver can insert the key token received from Llanrwst signal box and unlock the frame to change the points. Note the much narrower gauge Ffestiniog Railway track in the foreground and the station wall made of slate.

Blaenau Ffestiniog station is 27 miles 41 chains (44.3km) from Llandudno Junction.

Back on the main line towards Holyhead, the line continues along the coast past Conway station to the next stop, Penmaenmawr.

Fig. 140   Llanrwst signal box, January 2015.

Penmaenmawr (PR)

Date Built	1952
LNWR Type or Builder	BR LMR Type 14+
No. of Levers	25
Ways of Working	AB
Current Status	Active
Listed (Y/N)	N

Penmaenmawr is another holiday resort with a beach within walking distance of the station. It is less commercial than other resorts and appeals to walkers, hikers and campers, combining the virtues of spectacular mountains and coastal walks. The town is named after the mountain of that name close by.

For many years the town was much occupied with the quarrying of granite, and its proximity to the sea enabled a ready export path; a narrow gauge tramway helped in this endeavour. Later,

Fig. 141   Blaenau Ffestiniog station, April 2006.

Fig. 142   Penmaenmawr signal box, January 2015.

Fig. 143   Penmaenmawr looking towards Chester, January 2015.

when the railway arrived in 1848, sidings were constructed and railway wagons loaded direct from the granite crusher as railway track ballast. This continued until the 2000s but appears to have stopped now. The granite company here used to manufacture the 'setts', an early form of block paving, and examples of these in use can be found at Abergele and Llandudno stations.

Penmaenmawr shares one unfortunate attribute with Abergele – a mishap with the Irish Mail. In August 1950 the Irish Mail had left Holyhead for Euston and was approaching Penmaenmawr station at speed as the distant signal was set to clear. The signaller then threw the home signal in the train's path to danger, and although the Irish Mail crew braked it was too late to avoid a collision with a light engine that was stationary on the up line. Six people lost their lives.

Fig. 142 shows Penmaenmawr signal box. The sun shining in seems to be a problem here, as the windows were very much reduced in size in the 1990s from roof to ledge height to what is seen now. A photograph of the interior a few years ago revealed LNWR block instruments in use.

Fig. 143 shows the signal box and the up starter towards Chester, with the headshunt and main line connection to the ballast workings on the left.

Still looking towards Chester in Fig. 144, the station overview reveals some fine surviving station buildings that are in private hands now. On the left are the ballast sidings, beyond those the A55 road and further to the left the beach. The town is on the right and the Penmaenmawr mountain is on the far right.

Fig. 144   Penmaenmawr station looking towards Chester, January 2015.

Looking towards Bangor and Holyhead in Fig. 145, just beyond the station is Pen-y-Clip avalanche tunnel and Penmaenmawr viaduct. The building at the end of the up platform ramp is purported to have been a signal box at some point. The ballast sidings, latterly belonging to the Hanson company, do not seem to have been used for a while now but used to see class 40s and others heading ballast trains.

Penmaenmawr station is 228 miles and 69 chains (368.3km) from London Euston.

Bangor (BR)

Date Built	1923
LNWR Type or Builder	LNWR Type 5
No. of Levers	60
Ways of Working	AB
Current Status	Active
Listed (Y/N)	N

Bangor is an ancient city with its origins dating back to the sixth century. Nowadays, as well as being an administrative centre for the area, it is a university city, with the student population accounting for about 35 per cent of the total.

Bangor was an important railway junction, with lines to Caernarvon and Llanberis, for Snowdon, and connections to the Welsh Highland Railway. As well as a substantial station there was a steam loco-motive depot, coded 6H, extensive goods facilities and signal boxes.

In Fig. 146 Bangor signal box is still looking spruce after its 2009 refurbishment – it even has LNWR-type finials. This box had been Bangor No. 2 and even so has a reduced lever frame.

Fig. 145   Penmaenmawr looking towards Holyhead, January 2015.

Fig. 146   Bangor signal box, January 2015.

Bangor station throat looks towards Holyhead in Fig. 147, and the mechanical signalling on view is four ground discs. The sidings on the left just by the double-decker discs are all that is left of the exten-sive goods yard that was here. The double-track goods shed remains, albeit in other use. The tunnel

Fig. 147   Bangor station looking towards Holyhead, January 2015.

Fig. 148   Bangor station looking towards Chester, January 2015.

is the 648yd (593m) Belmont Tunnel; about a mile after that the line goes to single track briefly to cross the Menai Bridge to Anglesey and head onwards to Holyhead.

Bangor station platform 1 is shown in Fig. 148, and the Virgin Voyager 10 coach train has just started to move off but hasn't reached the green loop signal yet. The unit is bound for Chester and Euston.

There were tracks either side of the platforms, and the footbridge is a substantial one. The former steam depot is on the right, although the near end has been covered over with corrugated sheeting.

A call box on a station platform is a rarity and especially a 1930s art deco model, like the one at Bangor station shown in Fig. 149. A class 158, 158 835, is arriving at platform 2 with a stopping service to Holyhead. This time the platform dwarfs the train. The old steam depot is on the right and the train has just emerged from the 890yd (814m) Bangor Tunnel, complete with Egyptian-style portal.

Bangor station is 238 miles 71 chains (384.5km) from Euston station.

After we cross the Menai Strait to Anglesey, the first stop is a small station with a big name.

Fig. 149   Bangor station and engine shed, January 2015.

Anglesey is well known as a tourist destination and also had large employers in the shape of Anglesey Aluminium and Wylfa nuclear power station, both of which generated freight traffic for the line. There is still a freight presence from DRS, who run decommissioning trains for the nuclear power station.

Llanfair Level Crossing

Date Built	c.1871
LNWR Type or Builder	LNWR Type Chester and Holyhead Railway Panel
No. of Levers	
Ways of Working	Gate
Current Status	Active
Listed (Y/N)	N

Llanfairpwll, to use the shortened version, is the first station in Anglesey, and it has been restored in recent years by James Pringle weavers. The name was artificially concocted as a kind of early publicity stunt in the nineteenth century to attract tourists to the town. It has been remarkably successful and the name is known worldwide.

Llanfairpwllgwyngyllgogerychwyrndrobwllllantysiliogogogoch translates from the Welsh as: St Mary's church in the hollow of the white hazel near to the fierce whirlpool and the church of St Tysilio of the red cave. For brevity, it is often referred to as Llanfair PG.

The box, in Fig. 150, has only gate functions now – all signals are controlled from Bangor, which releases the locks on the gates to enable the signaller to move the gates manually to their new position. The box had originally been equipped with a gate wheel to open and close the gates from within the box.

The box is a picture in spring, with many plants and a small garden to the rear. The box is remarkably early and is thought to date from Chester and Holyhead Railway days before even the LNWR took the line over. When boxes are this old they tend not to have fully documented origins. The box originally had an eighteen-lever frame with a crossover and its own signals, and became a pivotal point after the Britannia Bridge fire in 1972. It was after that the line across the Menai Strait was reduced to single track.

The box is shown doing its job in Fig. 151, with the gates selected for road traffic. The road aperture is clearly smaller than the rail one, as a double set of gates is needed that overlap when in the rail position, and the targets and lights do not line up with the rails. In situations where the apertures are more or less the same, the lamp on top of the gates serves as a warning to rail traffic as well as road. There were two sets of lenses to give two separate indications.

The device inside the running rail on the left-hand up track is an additional locking device that senses the presence of a train and does not permit

Fig. 150   Llanfairpwllgwyngyllgogerychwyrndrobwllllantysiliogogogoch signal box, September 2005.

Fig. 151   Llanfair PG looking towards Chester, September 2005.

Fig. 152   Llanfair PG station, September 2005.

the gates to be opened while a train is approaching the crossing. The view is towards Bangor and Chester.

The restored station building with the name in full on the front is shown in Fig. 152. Platform tickets used to be required for anyone visiting a station platform and this station's platform tickets were sought after and sold for two and a half times the usual price.

The station name boards similarly attract the attentions of photographers, and coach parties visit the station in summer.

Llanfairpwllgwyngyllgogerychwyrndrobwllllantysiliogogogoch Level Crossing signal box is 242 miles and 22 chains (389.9km) from London Euston, and Llanfair PG station is 7 chains (140m) further on.

Gaerwen (GN)

Date Built	1882
LNWR Type or Builder	LNWR Type 4+
No. of Levers	20
Ways of Working	AB
Current Status	Active
Listed (Y/N)	N

Gaerwen is a village close to both major roads on Anglesey and is remarkable for having two disused windmills in the village. It was also the southern station of the Anglesey Central Railway to Amlwch, which is a port on the north of the island, some 17 miles (27km) away. Freight services survived until 1993.

Gaerwen had its own station and goods yard, and the site of these installations is where the parked cars are in Fig. 153. Signal boxes can be the focal point of small communities, and this box retains the Royal Mail post box. Although the box has been modernized on the first floor level, it is fairly original lower down and also retains vestiges of finials on the roof, as well as the bracket for the pot insulator telephone/telegraph wires on the right-hand side above the window.

Fig. 154 shows the view down the line towards Holyhead and the usual signals for down and up main lines. Off to the far right, however, is the exit signal for the 17 mile-plus (27km) Amlwch branch line. The point to connect the branch to the up main line has been removed but the branch track is still in position, just beyond the trailing crossover, as well as the point rodding and track-circuited ground signal for moves over it.

The view the other way, towards Chester, is shown in Fig.155, and while the up signal on the left has a track circuit lozenge, the down side does not. Note the W whistle board on the up side – the nomenclature is from steam days, as trains can no longer do whistling. The requirement to whistle or hoot is probably for Llandaniel crossing, which is classed as Miniature Warning Lights with Gates, user operated, and is 66 chains or 1,452yd (1,328m) from the box.

The other piece of the lever frame is through the locking frame window on the left (Fig. 156). This is an LNWR bar-and-stud type locking frame, but although there are different types and manufacturers of frames, they all operate on the same basic principle.

The signals and points are together in the same lever frame. The operation of a signal or point usually causes a lever to move in the frame to actuate the function. Into that lever are cut slots. Into these slots a bar or stud or lever can slide in at right angles to the original lever and this bar,

Fig. 154   Gaerwen and branch towards Holyhead, January 2015.

Fig. 153   Gaerwen signal box, January 2015.

Fig. 155   Gaerwen looking towards Chester, January 2015.

stud or lever is actuated by another point or signal. When this happens it is impossible to move the original lever.

This is the basic principle of a lock on a function. There can be several slots cut into a lever, into which several other points or signals levers can slot. Not all the interlocking in a signal box can be achieved this way, however, and we have already seen detection slides for points and ground discs at Crewe Steel Works in Fig. 73.

In addition there are electrical locks that force an electrical solenoid to lock the lever. It may be that the locking function is required from another signal box.

One of the levers in the frame has been pulled over and has a white counterbalance, which would tend to make the lever easier to pull over or reverse.

Towards the top of Fig. 156 there are levers to a series of grey boxes, which are switches – Gaerwen's two distant signals are both colour lights. The levers in the box attached to these will be of the cut-down type we saw at Prestatyn signal box in Fig. 98. The stout planks are for the signalling

Fig. 156   Gaerwen signal box locking room, January 2015.

technician to stand on to work on the frame. The chains are attached to signal pulleys.

Locking frame rooms can also have track circuit relays and other electronic communications equipment, such as routers, if there is room. If not, huts or Portakabins are usually provided outside the box.

Gaerwen signal box is 245 miles 9 chains (394.5km) from London Euston.

Tŷ Croes (TC)

Date Built	1872
LNWR Type or Builder	LNWR Type Chester and Holyhead Railway
No. of Levers	6
Ways of Working	Gate
Current Status	Active
Listed (Y/N)	Y

Tŷ Croes is a small village that was once home to an RAF Radar unit. It now has farms and camping holidays. In one location campers can enjoy a vineyard – the Gulf Stream washes this part of Britain and many places hereabouts benefit with better weather than the mainland.

Tŷ Croes is a really individual signal box, with no other like it on this line. One could sometimes find signal boxes and station buildings as one building in Scotland, but most of those have now gone. The box in Fig. 157 does look original, as befits a listed

Fig. 157 Tŷ Croes signal box, January 2015.

building; the windows were replaced in 1998 but still look the part.

The gates are operated by the signaller manually with only electrical locking. There are two home signals and two distants, one of which is a colour light signal, according to relatively recent diagrams. There are no block instruments here but usually there is some connection between block posts either side of the box and gate function.

The split platform layout of the station is evident in Fig. 158 and the crossing is the divisor. The waiting shelter on the right on the down side looks original but has a felt roof; this is platform 2. The crossing keeper's cottage is in private hands but is no doubt contemporary with the other buildings.

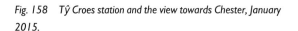

Fig. 158 Tŷ Croes station and the view towards Chester, January 2015.

Fig. 159 Tŷ Croes station with a class 175 arriving from Holyhead, January 2015.

Fig. 160 Tŷ Croes station with a class 175 bound for Chester, January 2015.

On platform 1, in Fig. 159, a class 175 Coradia, 175 109, from Holyhead is slowing down as it's been flagged down by a passenger as Tŷ Croes is a request stop. The cottage garden path is a right of way onto the platform, but it is lightly used.

The passenger is able to climb aboard in Fig. 160 without using the steps provided as the guard/conductor oversees the boarding and door closing. Early stations often have portable steps to compensate for the fact that modern rolling stock does not have the extensive footboards of early carriages,

which were themselves adaptations of horse-drawn carriages.

Tŷ Croes station platform 1 (up) is 254 miles 27 chains (409.3km) and platform 2 (down) 254 miles 34 chains (409.5km) from London Euston.

Valley (VY)

Date Built	1904
LNWR Type or Builder	LNWR Type 5
No. of Levers	25
Ways of Working	AB
Current Status	Active
Listed (Y/N)	Y

Valley is a village at a crossroads but is better known for the nearby RAF Valley, which, as well as being the RAF's Flying Training School, is also a search and rescue base. HRH the Duke of Cambridge spent some time on search and rescue duties at RAF Valley from 2010 to 2013 and lived with the Duchess at a rented property nearby.

Valley signal box (Fig. 161) is yet another listed LNWR signal box and the whole station area has a heritage feel to it. However, the VY 23 signal in front of the box is plated with the GSM-R telephone number for the box, which is a modern feature and has been missing from some signals on the line. The up platform ramp on the left is by the beginning of a special path to the box. This may indicate that

Fig. 161 Valley signal box, January 2015.

Fig. 162   Valley signal box and station building, January 2015.

Fig. 163   Rear of Valley signal box, January 2015.

the original occupant of the station building was a porter/signaller who looked after all the station and signal box work at quieter stations. Beyond the box on the up side, towards Chester, is the siding that leads to a loading siding and run-round loop for DRS trains to collect nuclear flasks from the Wylfa power station, which must be brought here by road. This probably explains why the ground disc at the foot of VY 23 is track circuited.

Fig. 162 shows the view towards Holyhead from across the crossing. The station building is unoccupied and boarded up although there are padlocks on the doors that have seen recent use so this may be a Network Rail store.

Fig. 164   Valley home signal looking towards Holyhead, January 2015.

The signaller's path can be clearly seen. The line curves around to the left and there is a crossover just by the end of the platform to enable the nuclear flask trains to cross over from the down line to the up to access the siding we saw in Fig. 161.

Fig. 163 shows the rear of Valley signal box. Note the window at the far end for keeping tabs on the traffic, complete with iron rail for leaning on. The green building next to the box is a lamp oil store, where oil lamps for all the signals could be filled up – once a week in more recent times, though in days of yore it was a daily chore.

Fig. 164 is included because the line curves round so the usual view of the outer home signal is lost. Signal VY 23 on the up side is looking at colour light VY 7 on the down, which is repeated to Holyhead as HD 115R, so the port is not far away now.

Valley station is 260 miles 9 chains (418.6km) from London Euston.

Holyhead (HD)

Date Built	1937
LNWR Type or Builder	LMS Type 11c+
No. of Levers	100
Ways of Working	AB
Current Status	Active
Listed (Y/N)	N

Holyhead is the largest town on Anglesey but is not actually on the island but on neighbouring Holy Island, which is connected to Anglesey via a causeway. Recently the A55 road has been upgraded to strengthen the link. Holyhead has been the port for departures to Ireland for as much as 4,000 years, historians suggest. It came to greater prominence after Thomas Telford built the post road from London to Holyhead – now the A5 – and mail coaches started using the road in the latter part of the eighteenth century.

The position was further strengthened by the Chester and Holyhead Railway, which was later taken over by the LNWR. Holyhead remains principal departure point for Ireland, with Stena Line and Irish Ferries both running services from here to Dublin.

Holyhead signal box (Fig. 165) is just over the road from McDonald's car park and the box may well qualify as a Big Mac in signal box terms. After Shrewsbury Severn Bridge Junction and Crewe Junction, it is the largest in terms of ex-LNWR lever count, if not in actual building size. Quite a lot of the original layout still exists, except that the original freight and loco depots are no longer with us. The loco depot, coded 6J, saw an allocation of Britannia Pacifics in later years as well as Duchess class locomotives as visitors, also in later years. Note that there is no point rodding coming out of the box at the front.

Much of the layout was photographed from three conveniently placed bridges, so what follows is a journey from the outskirts of Holyhead to the buffer stops at the ferry terminal station.

Fig. 166 shows the Holyhead station approaches looking towards Chester. Signal HD 86 has captions for three different subsidiary siding or loop destinations on it. The line on the left is the up main but is bi-directionally signalled at this point.

Note the very large water tower used in steam days, which is a typical LNWR example. Some contained coaling facilities underneath the water tower, and the coal train shunter would park inside in cold weather to stop the water tank from freezing up. The view is from the Cyttir Road overbridge. The view from the other side of the bridge is of a couple of crossovers until we come to the Penllech Nest footbridge.

Fig. 167 shows the Holyhead approaches from the Penllech Nest footbridge, with the down main on the far left and the up main next to it. The first signal is on the right just by the bridge and is a repeater that can show off; it refers to signal HD 91, which is a colour light on the up main on the right just beyond the first semaphore signal on the up main with its back to us. We can see the signal from our vantage point but train drivers obviously can't.

The colour light for the down main is much further down and on the left side of its track. The current loco depot and refuelling point is behind the

Fig. 165   Holyhead signal box, January 2015.

Fig. 166   Holyhead approaches looking towards Chester, January 2015.

Fig. 167　Holyhead signal box and loco depot, January 2015.

box where the steam shed was, and the exit signal is the furthest right of the semaphores. The roads in front of the box are for platform 3 at Holyhead station, to the left, and the one next to the box is the locomotive run-round for platform 3.

Back down to earth near McDonald's again, Fig. 168 is looking towards the station, with the box out of shot on the right.

From left to right the tracks are:

1. Shunting neck or headshunt, where the buffer stops are
2. Short siding so called, from which there is a further siding, called wall siding, beyond the bridge
3. Mail line
4. Carriage washing plant.
5. Platform 1 (which has a loco release loop but this is out of shot)
6. Platform 2 (there was a further platform next to 2 but that has no track now)
7. Platform 3
8. Loco release loop for platform 3.

Class 158 no. 158 835 is leaving from platform 2 and you can just see its starter off. Platform 3 starter is on the platform and its grey post can also just be seen. The train shed overall roof is on the right, on the skyline.

Fig. 168　Holyhead station throat, January 2015.

Fig. 169　Holyhead station throat looking towards Chester, January 2015.

Swinging round, with the box on the left now, the road is set in Fig. 169 for the class 158 to leave Holyhead on the up main, which is the second set of tracks from the gorse bush on the right and signal HD 39. Note how the two colour light signals with their backs to the camera have two and three caption boxes respectively below the lamp head for route describing, and below them an elevated electronic type of ground disc. The line from platform 3 joins the up main here, with the crossover in the foreground.

The signal on the left, HD 95, is the loco depot exit and the track rises up to go behind the box to the left.

The main line is curving to the left, as can be seen by the position of the LNWR water tower. The nearer bridge is the footbridge from Penllech Nest and beyond that is the Cyttir Road overbridge.

Holyhead station is also built on a curve. Fig. 170 shows the view from a side road off the London Road overbridge, and this road cuts the station platforms in two. On the left is platform 2, where the class 158 we saw in Fig. 169 set off from; on the right of that is what was a fourth platform but is now vacant of track; and beyond that, out in the cold outside the overall roof, is platform 3 with its associated loco run-round track. Near the end of platform 3 is a signal that is controlled by a ground frame off the end of the platform, together with the release crossover.

Fig. 170   Holyhead station overall roof, January 2015.

Platform 3 seen from the buffer stops in Fig. 171 shows the curious signal at the end of the platform with its ground frame. The unusual positioning of the signal may be as a result of a train driver wishing to join a ferry berthed nearby on a roll-on basis. Note how, at this earlier date, there was a crossover here and not just a loco release point as there is now.

In Fig. 172 a class 175 Coradia is departing from platform 2 and we can see the starter signal off past London Road bridge. The platform 3 starter is bracketed out, and over to the right is platform 1's starter. The cast iron Victorian lamp standard on

Fig. 171   Holyhead station platform 3 and ground frame, September 2005.

Fig. 172   Holyhead station with a class 175 departing towards Chester, January 2015.

the private road wall parapet does work. No space is wasted and in time-honoured fashion offices and stores sit underneath the arches – a sort of railway cupboard under the stairs.

Platform 1 and its starter signal are shown in Fig. 173. The signals, from top to bottom, are HD 35, HD 72 and HD 53. The top one is for trains departing on the up main towards Chester; below that is a calling on or shunt ahead arm to allow a train to proceed a little way for shunting; and the ground disc is for shunting locally. Platform 1 also has a ground frame at the loco release end but no signal at the end of the platform. Note how the extra unused doll on the bracket is used to tie the signal post to the roadway wall, which does not look inclined to go anywhere. Note also the Victorian block paving is still in situ on the platform.

Holyhead signal box is 263 miles and 26 chains (423.8km), and the station 263 miles 52 chains (424.3km) from London Euston.

Manchester to Buxton

Manchester achieved early prominence in the textile industry and was dubbed 'cottonopolis' as a result. The city subsequently diversified into heavy industry and manufacturing, with locomotives at Beyer Peacock and heavy electrical engineering with Associated Electrical Industries (AEI). The Manchester Ship Canal at Salford gave the

Fig. 173   Holyhead station platform 1, January 2015.

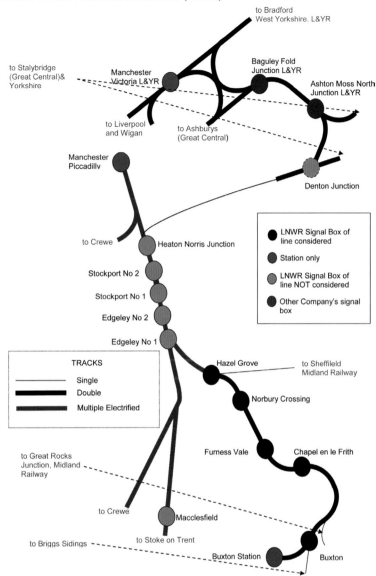

Fig. 174   Manchester–Buxton line schematic diagram.

cities ready access to markets as well as a throng of pre-grouping railway companies, of which the LNWR was one. As at Llandudno, some business-people lived outside the city, and the spa town of Buxton was a popular choice – so much so that the Midland Railway built a line there too. The LNWR passenger line survives but the Midland still goes to Buxton, though much of it is now freight only. *See* Volume 1 for the former Midland Railway in that area.

The simplified schematic diagram in Fig. 174 has included other signal boxes that are not part of this journey but are included for contextual purposes. The railway scene in Manchester is still a complex one, with deep historical roots, if not routes.

Hazel Grove (HG)

Date Built	*c.*1877
LNWR Type or Builder	LNWR Type 4
No. of Levers	OCS panel
Ways of Working	AB
Current Status	Active
Listed (Y/N)	N

As well as being a better-heeled suburb of Stockport, Greater Manchester, Hazel Grove has a manufacturing presence in the electronics industry, and formerly ethical drugs as well. It is a terminus on the tram system, and the 25kV overhead electrified tracks from Manchester Piccadilly also terminate here.

After the line was electrified from Stockport Edgeley Junction to Hazel Grove in 1981, Hazel Grove (Fig. 175) was retained as it acts as 'fringe' box to absolute block lines on the former Midland Railway route to Sheffield and the ex-LNWR route to Buxton. A one control switch, or OCS panel, contains a number of single switches that can set a route by themselves for a train to take. There is one switch for each route. There are separate switches for points, however, so that an individual selection can be made, but they are generally left in the automatic position for OCS operation.

In Fig. 176 Pacer class 142 045, bound for Manchester Piccadilly, is arriving at the platform. The 142 and 153 classes are prohibited from working the Buxton line because of the steep gradients, so this unit must have originated in Sheffield. The ex-Midland Railway branch to the Hope Valley and Sheffield veers off to the left behind the Pacer, and the Buxton branch takes off to the right. The Midland Railway had its own station until 1917 but it was inconveniently situated and this hastened its closure.

Hazel Grove station and signal box are 2 miles 30 chains (3.8km) from Edgeley Junction.

Norbury Crossing

Date Built	1974
LNWR Type or Builder	BR London Midland Region Type 15+
No. of Levers	6
Ways of Working	Gate
Current Status	Active
Listed (Y/N)	N

Norbury Crossing is also known as Norbury Hollow, or possibly Leafy Hollow, as the box has left suburban Manchester behind and is right in the countryside. Sleepy Hollow it is not, though, with forty-three trains passing a day.

Paradoxically, we have moved from a box that was over 130 years old with fairly modern equipment to one forty years old with less modern equipment.

Norbury Crossing has manually operated gates and the box has survived because the road curves around, and consequently it is difficult to operate the crossing with CCTV.

Fig. 177 shows a fairly modern-looking building with modern protection on the windows. The road comes down on the left of the picture and curves round to cross right by the side of the box – many

Fig. 175 Hazel Grove signal box, July 2005.

Fig. 176 Hazel Grove station, July 2005.

Fig. 177   Norbury Crossing signal box, August 2006.

Fig. 178   Norbury Crossing signal box gates and signal, August 2006.

a signaller must have thought that sooner or later a motorist coming down the hill would make an unscheduled visit to the box.

Fig. 178 is the box from the side, and now the road is right behind the camera. The gate post for latching the gate to on this side of the road when a train is coming is on the extreme right of the picture – that's how sharp the bend is.

Some cultivation is taking place, with a hanging basket and planter tubs.

Inside the box is the simplest of diagrams (Fig. 179). Diagrams often make no attempt to show line curvature, and so it is here, though the gradient profile is in place. The two colour lights on the up line to Buxton are plated Hazel Grove, but Norbury must pull lever 2 before the signal nearest the crossing comes off. The signals on the down side towards Hazel Grove are both semaphores and the distant is motor worked, although it does not give distances. They are levers 3 and 4 in the frame respectively. Lever 5 is the brown gate lock lever. The distant signal has an enunciator to warn of an approaching train and this is reflected on the down line instrument attached to the front of

Fig. 179   Norbury Crossing signal box interior diagram and block shelf, August 2006.

Fig. 180   Norbury Crossing signal box lever frame, August 2006.

the shelf. There are no block instruments here so there is no signaller giving Norbury Train on Line from their instrument. The up line instrument has lost its label. Both indicators are showing Train in Section.

The six-lever frame with its LNWR stirrup-handled levers is shown in Fig. 180. Numbers 1 and 6 are not used, and 2 and 4 are a colour light signal and a motorized semaphore respectively, so have cut-down levers. The only true wire-worked signal is no. 3, which is the down home pictured outside the box in Fig. 178. The brown lever 5 is in the gates unlocked position. The ivorine lead plate on lever 6 lever requires that levers 26, 25, 24, 18 and 17 are pulled first. Clearly this has come from somewhere else and is a leg pull.

Norbury Crossing is 3 miles 60 chains (6km) from Stockport Edgeley Junction.

Furness Vale

Date Built	c.1887
LNWR Type or Builder	LNWR Type 4+
No. of Levers	22
Ways of Working	AB
Current Status	Active
Listed (Y/N)	N

We now leave Greater Manchester and arrive in Derbyshire at Furness Vale in the High Peak. Furness Vale, although it is small village, is somewhat of a transport crossroads, with the A6 road, Peak Forest Canal and railway complete with station.

In Fig. 181 the box is in recognizably original condition despite uPVC windows and bricked-up locking frame windows. The Furness Vale plate on the box end is an enamelled sign that harks back to London Midland Region days and is maybe fifty to sixty years old. They are prized as collector's items, their value closely related to location – the more exotic the better – and ones from closed boxes are also more sought after. The box has two BR domino block instruments for Hazel Grove and Chapel-en-le-Frith, the next box towards Buxton.

Fig. 181   Furness Vale signal box, October 2014.

Fig. 182 is looking back towards Hazel Grove. The trailing crossover near the pair of signals has just one ground disc for reversing from the down left-hand track to the up right-hand track.

The rodding is on its way on the left side of the track, and this is slightly odd as there are two rods for the crossover whereas the norm is only one, and the movement of both points is usually conveyed by further rodding. There is no facing point lock here either.

Fig. 183 shows Furness Vale station platforms and the line heading off towards Buxton. The footbridge survives and is an LNWR original. In addition to the five signals seen here, there are two semaphore distant signals.

Fig. 182   Furness Vale looking towards Hazel Grove, July 2005.

Fig. 183   *Furness Vale looking towards Buxton, July 2005.*

Fig. 184   *Chapel-en-le-Frith signal box, October 2014.*

Furness Vale station is 8 miles 62 chains (14.1km) from Edgeley Junction and at an altitude of 540ft (165m).

Chapel-en-le-Frith (CH)

Date Built	1957
LNWR Type or Builder	BR London Midland Region Type 15+
No. of Levers	20
Ways of Working	AB
Current Status	Active
Listed (Y/N)	N

Chapel-en-le-Frith is an ancient and attractive market town that still holds weekly markets on a cobbled street. It has been dubbed the 'Capital of the Peaks' as a centre for visitors and tourists. It also has the Federal Mogul factory, which manufactures car parts.

Chapel-en-le-Frith signal box is shown in Fig. 184 together with a pair of its signals and some hanging basketry on the station platforms; the view is looking towards Buxton. The signal box is relatively modern and is a replacement for a box that was demolished by a runaway train.

In February 1957 a freight train with ex-LMS 2–8–0 steam locomotive no. 48188 was being banked in the rear up a steep gradient a few miles outside Buxton. A catastrophic failure of a steam joint engulfed the loco cab in scalding steam. After the loco reached the summit, even though some of the wagon brakes were pinned down, the train began to run away downhill, and despite valiant efforts to close the regulator and bring the train to a halt it continued to accelerate downhill. The driver told the fireman to jump off and try to pin down more wagon brakes and advise the guard of their predicament.

The driver stayed with the train and it eventually collided with the rear of another freight train in the next section at Chapel-en-le-Frith station. The 775-ton train plus locomotive made short work of the signal box and much of the station. The guard of the stationary freight train, John Creamer, was killed, as was the driver of the runaway freight train, John Axon.

John Axon was posthumously awarded the George Cross. He also had a locomotive and a DMU train named after him.

Fig. 185 shows the station platform ends towards Hazel Grove. The need for the Whistle sign is for an ungated crossing about 40 yards from the platform end. Note the yellow quarter-mile marker post on the right-hand up side. Chapel-en-le-Frith also has the former Midland Railway route running close by, though this is now a freight-only line to Peak Forest and Great Rocks Junction – *see* Volume 1 for details.

Fig. 185   Chapel-en-le-Frith looking towards Hazel Grove, October 2014.

Fig. 186   Chapel-en-le-Frith station, October 2014.

The former Midland Railway monolithic goods shed is at Chapel and is now a builder's merchant.

Fig. 186 offers an overview of the station, looking towards Buxton again. The station building has a blue plaque that commemorates the actions of John Axon GC and John Creamer. The station is unusual in that passengers are required to cross the line to reach the far platform, as there is no footbridge here.

The station building is also home to the Brief Encounter café, which is presently undergoing refurbishment. They had all manner of railway artefacts on display at the original survey date.

Chapel-en-le-Frith station is 13 miles 67 chains (22.3km) from Stockport Edgeley Junction.

Buxton

Date Built	c.1894
LNWR Type or Builder	LNWR Type 4+
No. of Levers	45
Ways of Working	AB
Current Status	Active
Listed (Y/N)	N

Buxton was known for its spa water since Roman times but was developed by the Duke of Devonshire, from nearby Chatsworth House, with many fine neo-classical buildings from the late eighteenth

century. Buxton is the highest market town in England and is a sought-after residential address, with its Pavilion Gardens and opera house.

The railway companies were quick to see business in Buxton, and the LNWR and the Midland Railway both built branch lines from Manchester and ran commuter trains. Two very similar stations were established at Buxton right next to each other to minimize the impact on the town, and their design and location were approved by the Duke of Devonshire. Only the LNWR passenger station survives although the Midland Railway lines continue with freight traffic.

As with Holyhead, the approach here will be to begin at the railway outskirts and progress to the

Fig. 187   Buxton approaches with the view towards Hazel Grove, February 2015.

terminus station buffer stops. There are two freight branch lines on the way.

Fig. 187 is the approach from Chapel-en-le-Frith, and from Furness Vale the line has climbed almost 500ft (150m). The home signal on the up right-hand line has a yellow quarter-mile post near it, which declares 18 and two spots, where each spot is one quarter mile: this point is 18½ miles (29.8km) from Edgeley Junction at Stockport. Note how the small posts carrying the signal wire stand out, and the sleepers piled up along the trackside for a renewal exercise at some point.

Fig. 188 is looking the other way, from the Brown Edge Road footbridge towards the box and station. The double tracks continue to curve round into the station accompanied by the pile of sleepers, and we are informed by another quarter-mile post that it is 18¾ miles (30.2km) from Edgeley Junction. The box is very handily placed in that the three lines that meet at Buxton are by the box. Apart from the passenger lines to the station, to the right is a single-track branch behind the box and just visible in the snow; this leads to Brigg's Sidings, which is a quarry complex.

To the left of and in front of the box is another single-track branch that leads to Great Rocks Junction and Chinley and the Midland route to Manchester and Sheffield. The purpose of the tracks where the seven ground discs are, on the left, is to enable a train to arrive from Brigg's Sidings, run into a loop then run round and set off facing the opposite way to go to Great Rocks Junction and beyond.

The home signal on the left-hand up side protects the station and has a calling on arm beneath the main arm. This is to caution a train to run into a platform that may already be occupied. This calling on arm is in action later – *see* Fig. 193.

Buxton signal box is in Siberian winter camouflage in Fig. 189. As with many other busy boxes, the emphasis is on an efficient and safe working environment rather than concern over the aesthetics.

The line around the back of the box to Brigg's Sidings is clearly visible, as is the branch to Great Rocks Junction, which has its entry and exit signals in view to the left.

Fig. 188   Buxton approaches with the view towards Buxton, February 2015.

Fig. 189   Buxton signal box, February 2015.

Buxton to Brigg's Sidings is worked no signaller key token, which means the only signaller-worked key token apparatus is at the box. The train driver has to operate the token apparatus down the branch, if there is one, as well as use the key token to unlock and operate ground frames.

Buxton to Great Rocks Junction is key token, where there are token apparatus and signallers at both ends.

In Fig. 190 the driver of class 66 loco 66 020 surrenders the token to the signaller from the Brigg's Sidings NSKT section. The train will then draw forward into the loop for the locomotive to run round; then, after collecting a different token for the section ahead, it will drive off to Great Rocks Junction.

Fig. 190   Buxton signal box; the signaller collects the key token from the class 66 driver, February 2015.

Fig. 191   Buxton run-round loop for Great Rocks Junction, February 2015.

Looking the other way in Fig. 191, we can see where the class 66 is headed – the complicated piece of track in the middle of the picture is a single slip. This achieves the same as a diamond crossing but with the addition that it lets one set of track continue straight on, as it were. The loco is coming up from the third set of tracks from the bottom. It will then be switched by the signaller to remain on the third track up. Had this been a simple diamond crossing, the train would have ended up on the fourth track over by the green fence, but this is just the run-round loop. Single slips are quite rare outside large stations but are useful, as they save space. The down side is they can only be traversed at low speed so are no use for running lines.

In Fig. 192 loco 66 020, still in EWS livery at this late date, takes the crossover to lead onto the single slip seen in Fig. 191. The train, which must weigh about 1,500 tonnes, just fits into the run round loop.

The Northern Rail class 150, loco 150 228, passes the home signal seemingly at danger until it is realized that the train has been cautioned and allowed to proceed slowly into the platform by the calling on arm, which is off. We saw these signals in Figs. 188 and 191.

In Fig. 194 we are on platform 2 at Buxton station. Moving to the left, there is a carriage siding then platform 1. On the extreme left is the disused diesel motive power depot. The storage tanks for refuelling are still in place out of shot behind platform 1. Both platform starter signals are on view and platform 1's is bracketed out and lower than its neighbour because of the overall roof. The Joseph

Fig. 192   A class 66 at Buxton heads for the run-round loop, February 2015.

Fig. 193 A DMU at Buxton passes the calling on signal, February 2015.

Fig. 194   Buxton station and loco depot, February 2015.

Fig. 195   Buxton station, July 2005.

Paxton-designed station used to have an attractive overall roof that, while lacking the grandeur of Paxton's Crystal Palace, was a landmark in the town together with its Midland Railway neighbour right next door.

Fig. 195 is from an earlier time but demonstrates the working of a class 150 DMU into a platform already occupied by another DMU. The yellow vehicle next to the DMU is a track-maintenance vehicle. The fanlight effect of Paxton's gable end

Fig. 196   Buxton station with class 150s, February 2015.

roof is in evidence, as is the wall coming out at right angles from the left. This is one of the overall roof supports. The station canopy on platform 2 is a later addition. The station is Grade II listed.

Fig. 196 is a more up-to-date shot although not much has changed except that the station appears tidier and there are fewer weeds. The class 150 we saw passing the calling on arm has been moved across from platform 2 to the disused platform 1.

Buxton signal box is 18 miles 70 chains (30.4km) from Stockport Edgeley Junction.

Wirral and Runcorn

The Wirral landscape contrasts an industrial port scene on the banks of the River Mersey with a more pastoral and upmarket residential one mostly towards the River Dee estuary, where the vista is towards the hills of north Wales.

The Wirral, as part of the county of Chester, attracted early interest and jostling from railway companies to establish a presence there. The LNWR was the main winner out of all the smaller concerns but found itself aligned with the GWR in the peninsula. This narrow isthmus between the rivers Dee and Mersey also played host to the Great Central Railway, who were to become part of the London and North Eastern Railway. In this geographically unlikely part of the country three of the big four companies fought it out for access to the ports of the River Mersey and to service the Liverpool commuter land that had been invented by rail travel.

The only vestiges of railway mechanical signalling that survive are from the LNWR, and some of that is isolated in pockets.

This is due to two factors. The first is the electrification and modernization of the Liverpool main line area, and second is the similar electrification and modernization of Merseyrail, though using a different system, to meet the needs of a busy suburban and metropolitan network.

Runcorn is a port on the River Mersey and has large chemical works, some of which is rail served. Runcorn is on the main line to Liverpool Lime Street and the station is a hub for passengers travelling outside the region.

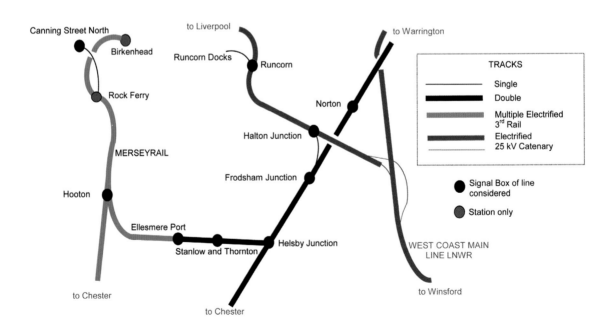

Fig. 197 Wirral and Runcorn area schematic diagram.

The journey begins at Runcorn and travels south and across to the Merseyrail area before ending at Birkenhead.

Runcorn (RN)

Date Built	1940
LNWR Type or Builder	LMS Type 13
No. of Levers	45
Ways of Working	TCB, OTW
Current Status	Active
Listed (Y/N)	Y

Runcorn wasn't much more than a village until the coming of the railway. The narrowing of the River Mersey at the Runcorn Gap provided the LNWR with the ideal place to bridge the river. The Runcorn Bridge, built in 1868, is still a magnificent structure at 915yd (837m) long and is Grade II listed. The bridge also crosses the Manchester Ship Canal, which wasn't built until many years afterwards, and the Bridgewater Canal that preceded it.

Runcorn signal box in Fig. 198 is one of the first boxes built by the LMS under the wartime Air Raid Precautions or ARP regulations. The 14in-thick (35cm) walls and 12in-thick (30cm) concrete roof are designed to withstand bomb blast damage but clearly not a direct hit. The metal window frames were also designed to be better than wood as it was thought they would not splinter if bomb blasted. Timber was scarce during World War II and early concrete sleepers replaced wood.

The original LNWR box at Runcorn had been a wooden one on stilts, but while it provided good all-round visibility, the rodding and signal wires coming down from the box were vulnerable to bomb damage, as was as the box itself.

As an early example of the ARP style, Runcorn was Grade II listed in 2013.

The box works one train working down the Folly Lane branch to Runcorn Docks. This branch had

originally serviced the ICI chemical works, later Ineos Chlor, and now sees about three trains a day going to a recycling plant.

OTW operates on the principle of the branch signal acting as the authority for the train to proceed. The entry signal is then locked to further access until the returning train operates two track circuits on the way back. The train can then leave the branch and another can be admitted. The single-track branch has sidings and a run-round loop.

Runcorn signal box is 180 miles 33 chains (290.3km) from London Euston.

Halton Junction (HN)

Date Built	1897
LNWR Type or Builder	LNWR Type 4
No. of Levers	25
Ways of Working	TCB, AB
Current Status	Active
Listed (Y/N)	N

Travelling south from Runcorn we encounter Halton Junction, which sees the electrified main line continue south to join up with the WCML, all track circuit block worked. A single-track branch leaves here for Frodsham Junction but this single-track line is one-directional – trains only run from Frodsham to Halton Junction.

Halton Junction signal box in Fig. 199 even has diamond-pattern replacement roof tiles to complete the image of a refurbished box.

Fig. 198   Runcorn signal box, March 2006.

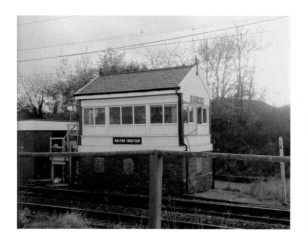

Fig. 199   Halton Junction signal box, November 2014.

Fig. 200   Halton Junction signal box, October 2007.

The single-track branch to Frodsham heads off behind the box.

Fig. 200 is a pre-refurbishment view of Halton Junction signal box. Note the period galvanised dustbins and a stone structure on the right of the box, and the older-style metal staircase.

The quarter-mile post is confirmation that the box is 179 miles 20 chains (290.3km) from London Euston.

Frodsham Junction (FJ)

Date Built	*c.*1894
LNWR Type or Builder	LNWR Type 5+
No. of Levers	32
Ways of Working	AB
Current Status	Active
Listed (Y/N)	N

Frodsham is an attractive and popular market town that benefited from river traffic on the Weaver Navigation. Before that it was an important location that received patronage from the Earls of Chester. Its station was built in 1849 and was an early contributor to the Birkenhead Joint Railway before it came under the LNWR umbrella. The ornate station building is Grade II listed.

Fig. 201 is Frodsham box on its perch, which is a high embankment to run up to the bridge to clear the River Weaver, or more likely, the masts of sailing boats. The single line from Halton Junction runs in behind the box. As it is one-directional towards Halton Junction, there is no token or staff kit needed here. The double-track main line runs in front of the box, to the left is Helsby Junction, southwards, and to the right Runcorn East station and Norton signal box, our next stop. Frodsham Junction still has its dustbin and coal bunker where a four-wheel wagon would have its side door opened and resting on top of the bunker wall. This made it easy to shovel the box's supply of signaller coal into the bunker.

Fig. 201   Frodsham signal box, December 2014.

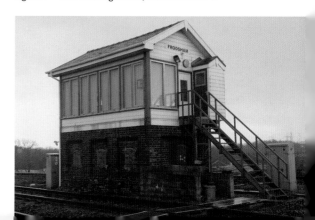

Fig. 202   Frodsham and Runcorn single line, December 2014.

Fig. 202 shows the double track crossing the River Weaver heading to Runcorn East, to the left. The branch for Halton Junction is signalled off the down main line by the junction signals in much the same LNWR way as we saw at Abergele. The catch points, so signed, are unusual in that they are 'worked', or lever switched, as opposed to the more usual spring-loaded version. Their purpose is to derail runaway wagons that are going in a direction contrary to that intended. They would be placed at the bottom of inclines, where loose-coupled goods trains would often break couplings, and the runaways would be derailed rather than meet a following train in collision.

All coaches and wagons are now supposed to have their brakes automatically applied if uncoupled from a train, but there are such things as ganger's trolleys that are not so equipped.

The function here would be to derail any runaway vehicle, but the points can also be lever operated to allow a train to travel in the opposite direction. Any derailment here, and the vehicles would come down the steep embankment. The bridge over the River Weaver is where the white railings trackside are and Frodsham station is over a mile (1.6km) further on by the town. Beacon or Frodsham Hill, which overlooks the town, is in the background.

In Fig. 203 the box is switched out. The view is towards Helsby Junction and, through the 87yd (80m) tunnel, Frodsham station. The up goods loop is on the left. The subsidiary smaller armed signal to let a train out of the loop has the track circuit lozenge on it, so presumably passenger trains can go in the loop. The trap points, by the loop signal post, are to derail vehicles running away in the normal direction of travel and are always lever worked and usually co-acting with the exit point or turnout.

Fig. 204 is the view from Halton Station Road overbridge and shows the up goods loop in its entirety. Note that there is a catch point on the loop by the near signal post. These points are spring-loaded in contrast to the worked catch points we saw in Fig. 202.

In Fig. 205 the reason for the name Halton Station in Fig. 204 becomes clear, with the remains of a platform on the up side and the station building of

Fig. 203   Frodsham and the view across Weaver Viaduct towards Helsby Junction, December 2014.

Fig. 204 (left)   Frodsham and a view of the goods loop and box, December 2014.

Fig. 205 (above)   Frodsham and the former Halton station, December 2014.

the name in use as a private residence. The bracket signal controls entry into the goods loop.

Frodsham signal box is dually distanced, in that it is 11 miles 9 chains (17.9km) from Chester and 1 mile 50 chains (2.6km) from Halton Junction.

At this point we continue the journey northwards to Norton, which is back up the line towards Runcorn and the East station.

Norton (NN)

Date Built	1972
LNWR Type or Builder	BR London Midland Region Type 15+
No. of Levers	10
Ways of Working	AB, TCB
Current Status	Active
Listed (Y/N)	N

Norton operates as a fringe box to the TCB area of Warrington power box as well as AB to Frodsham Junction southwards. The box controls a trailing crossover that does not have ground discs for reversing moves, so would appear to be hand signal worked and therefore seldom used.

Fig. 207 shows the Norton station building, which closed in 1952, on the down side towards the

Warrington end. It retains a Norton station 'target' sign although in private use. The sign is affixed to a modern extension but occupies the site of the ticket office and waiting room.

The signaller still gains access for car parking and a walkway across the tracks to get to work. The current Runcorn East station, pictured near the box, opened in 1983.

Norton signal box is 13 miles 17 chains (21.3km) from Chester.

Fig. 206   Norton signal box, January 2006.

Fig. 207 (above)   Runcorn East station, January 2006.

Fig. 208 (right)   Helsby Junction signal box, December 2014.

Helsby Junction (HY)

Date Built	1900
LNWR Type or Builder	LNWR Type 4
No. of Levers	45
Ways of Working	AB
Current Status	Active
Listed (Y/N)	Y

Helsby, like Frodsham, has ancient historic roots and similarly the village is overlooked by a large red sandstone hill, Helsby Hill. However, the local nabob here was the Marquis of Cholmondley. There was a considerable manufacturing presence here with British Insulated Callender's Cables (BICC) employing up to 5,000 people. The red sandstone was quarried at Mountskill and the quarry had an early tramway to get the stone to the River Mersey for onward transportation. The stone was used in prominent buildings in Birkenhead.

The station has survived intact from earliest times and is looked after by local volunteers. It has won Best Kept Station awards several times. The signal box is similarly well looked after and was listed in 2013.

Platform-mounted boxes, like Helsby Junction (Fig. 208), are not common. The tunnel for the rodding and signal wires is clearly in use. The amenity block on the end is the only real deviation from a well-preserved box, though the cage to ward off intruders is another modernistic addition.

The box is festooned with honours and the station reflects the judge's opinions. The blue plaque on the box front is an award by Westinghouse Ltd to Network Rail in 2004 and presented by HRH the Duke of Gloucester.

The box is situated on an island platform, with the line from Hooton behind the box and Chester in front.

Fig. 209 shows the junction arrangements at Helsby. The two lines on the left are heading off to Chester and the two on the right to Hooton. The footbridge joining up the platforms has an impact on the sighting of some of the signals, as we shall see later. The platforms are numbered – from left to right – 1, 2, 3, 4. The Birkenhead Joint Railway buildings, which are Grade II listed, can just be seen. The BJR was taken over by the LNWR in 1860.

Fig. 209   Helsby Junction, December 2014.

Fig. 210   Helsby Junction station looking towards Chester, December 2014.

In Fig. 210 class 158 loco 158 829 is coasting into platform 2 from Chester.

The sidings just where the DMU is were originally exchange sidings for the interchange of traffic that occurred at junctions. There is now a refuge siding, an engineer's siding and one remaining exchange siding. The single slip allows access to both siding groups, much as we saw at Buxton.

Just beyond the headshunt buffer stops by the platform is the name of Helsby set out in white-washed stones. The gardens too are a delight

Fig. 211   Helsby Junction station looking towards Ellesmere Port, December 2014.

and a credit to the volunteers. Such features were commonplace up until the 1960s at many country stations.

Fig. 211 is the view from the footbridge up the line to Hooton, with platform 4 on the right and platform 3 on the left. Platform 4 is bi-directionally signalled.

Note the island platform building has survived from Birkenhead Railway days. The tidy gardens and tubs are provided by the volunteers. About half a mile (1km) up the line towards Hooton is a crossover and private sidings complex belonging to Kemira Growhow.

Fig. 212 shows the lines up to Frodsham Junction, with Helsby's junction behind the camera. Note the lattice post component to the taller Chester signal and the shorter Hooton signal off the junction, as well as the LNWR-esque tie rod between them. At the survey date both posts had calling on arms below the main ones, which have subsequently been removed.

Fig. 213 shows a signalling oddity not much seen any longer. We have already come across banner repeater signals where the actual signal is repeated by another device. This time the signal arm is repeated by another signal arm, and in fact they are linked together. The double-armed signal on the left is platform 4's starter signal; the footbridge impedes the view of the lower arm so it is repeated and can be seen above the footbridge from some

Fig. 212   Helsby Junction station showing the Frodsham line signals, November 2004.

Fig. 213   Helsby Junction station and the Frodsham line platform starter signals, December 2014.

Fig. 214   Helsby Junction station overview, December 2014.

way off. Close to, the footbridge obscures the upper arm. The HY 37 home signal is platform 2's starter. Note the limit of shunt indicator between the two signal posts. This is the demarcation point beyond which no train that is shunting may go. The view in Fig. 212 was taken from the overbridge in the background, while the view here is towards Frodsham Junction.

Fig. 214 gives an overview of the box and station buildings from the footbridge. Chester direction is to the left, Hooton to the right.

However, our journey continues from platform 3 for Stanlow and Thornton, and beyond that to Hooton.

Helsby Junction station is 7 miles 34 chains (11.9km) from Chester station.

Stanlow and Thornton

Date Built	1941
LNWR Type or Builder	LMS Type 4
No. of Levers	50
Ways of Working	AB
Current Status	Demolished 2008
Listed (Y/N)	N

The station of the name opened at the end of 1940, and the site was much engaged in research into fuels and lubricants for RAF aircraft. The site developed into the Stanlow oil refinery, owned by Shell and now Essar. There was a large complex of loops and sidings to accommodate refinery traffic but the last train of refinery products left the yard in 1998. The yard had been one of the busiest in the north-west, with tanker trains arriving and departing day and night from all parts of the country. Recent years have seen the construction of pipelines, which have generally reduced tanker traffic.

The station is still open but for security reasons the private road to access the station is closed to the public. Nevertheless passenger traffic per year has risen from 40 in 2004/5 to 468 in 2011/2.

In Fig. 215 the signal box has lost its name board, a sure sign of impending doom. The box is in almost original condition except for the right-hand end front window; it is likely the locking frame windows were never fitted, given the date of the build.

However, the lever frame and furniture from the box was donated to the Embsay and Bolton Abbey Steam Railway in Yorkshire, so some of it lives on.

Signal boxes of this type were kept at Crewe in kit form ready to be wheeled out in case of bomb damage to existing structures. Most of the siding network was still in place at the survey date but overgrown and disused for some years before that, and the box had been switched out for years. Some of Stanlow's storage tanks are in the background.

Stanlow and Thornton station is 5 miles 67 chains (9.4km) from Hooton station, and the mileages from here on are now calculated this way.

Ellesmere Port (EP)

Date Built	1972
LNWR Type or Builder	BR London Midland Region Type 15+
No. of Levers	64
Ways of Working	AB, TCB
Current Status	Active
Listed (Y/N)	N

Ellesmere Port became such when the Ellesmere Canal reached the River Mersey. This pre-railway trading link established a waterways base that now

Fig. 215   Stanlow and Thornton signal box, October 2005.

Fig. 216   Ellesmere Port signal box, January 2015.

Fig. 217 Ellesmere Port signal box and station looking towards Hooton, January 2015.

forms part of the National Waterways Museum. At the turn of the nineteenth century the Manchester Ship Canal was built and Ellesmere Port further enhanced its water transport system with extensive docks and wharves, but this time fully rail supported. As with most ports on the west side of Britain, Ellesmere Port saw a decline in waterborne traffic but is now enjoying a resurgence, with imported coal for Fiddlers Ferry power station near Warrington.

Ellesmere Port is perhaps better known in recent times for the Astra factory of Vauxhall Motors and the Cheshire Oaks retail village.

Fig. 216 shows that there were several signal boxes here once, and this one is No. 4. The wisdom or otherwise of the flat roof is clear to see, with a pool of water collecting on the front that inevitably leads to a leak. Note the mass of signal wires gathered up in the trunking to go over the bridge and the group of point rodding heading the other way.

In Fig. 217 Ellesmere Port station is in the background, up the line towards Hooton. At the platforms, on the inside of the main running lines can be seen the third rail of the Merseyrail system, which terminates here, and trains can only occupy the right-hand platform. Electric trains regain the up left-hand main to Hooton by a crossover.

The station is straddled by two large yards to service the docks, chemical plant and part of Stanlow refinery. There is one that leaves the main line right after the platform end, on the right, and the other is accessed by the crossover in the foreground. The crossover into the yard looks well used despite the jungle.

Fig. 218 is looking back towards Helsby Junction, with the yard to the left of the main running lines. The birch trees are making their presence felt. Down the line are two subsidiary exit signals for the yard as well as an outer home with sighting board. Plenty of chemical works are in evidence. The red sandstone outcrop that forms Frodsham and Helsby hills is in the background.

In Fig. 219 Merseyrail class 507 EMU 507 031 waits to depart towards the camera for Hooton. The

Fig. 218 Ellesmere Port sidings and yard looking towards Helsby Junction, January 2015.

Fig. 219   Ellesmere Port station looking towards Helsby Junction, September 2005.

crossover for the train to get on the correct running line is just past the platform. The fine pre-LNWR Birkenhead Railway station building is Grade II listed. Northern Rail trains from Warrington Bank Quay station terminate here, so Ellesmere Port is the interface between two systems.

Fig. 220 shows the approaches to the second of the two yards referred to in Fig. 217. The left-hand track leads to Manisty Wharf, where coal and biomass pellets, imported from the USA, are unloaded, and where the Manchester Ship Canal Ellesmere Port loco shed was. To the right the tracks lead off to a further dock siding.

From here the track belongs to the Manchester Ship Canal company but the sign with the cross on it is a Network Rail trackside sign for a level crossing, of which there are many hereabouts. The check rails on both tracks are typical of sharply curved

dock lines. The red signal does not look like a Network Rail one.

There were two further tracks between the two shown and they fade out and reappear concreted into the roadway. The Manchester Ship Canal precedes the River Mersey in the background.

Ellesmere Port station is 3 miles 44 chains (5.7km) from Hooton station.

Hooton (HN)

Date Built	1985
LNWR Type or Builder	BR London Midland Region Presco structures
No. of Levers	Nx panel
Ways of Working	TCB, AB
Current Status	Active
Listed (Y/N)	N

Hooton is a pleasant village that has seen growth thanks to the railway. As well as the line from Helsby, Hooton is on the Chester–Birkenhead route and was also the junction for the line to West Kirby. The latter line closed some years ago but the track bed has been transformed into the Wirral Way for walkers and cyclists. Hooton therefore is a natural commuting base for many, and the station is busy.

Fig. 221 shows that Hooton signal box is a couple of Presco buildings stacked one upon the other. The Portakabin style of architecture for signal

Fig. 220   Ellesmere Port running lines to private sidings and docks, January 2015.

Fig. 221   Hooton signal box, January 2015.

Fig. 222   Hooton station looking towards Helsby and Chester, January 2015.

boxes has only utility and economy to commend it. The purpose of buildings like these is to give due warning that it will all be like this one day and then stiffen the resolve to prevent it. Still, these buildings will have their fans, and to see beauty in something can only enhance life generally.

In the middle distance two tracks lead off to Helsby Junction and beyond that two tracks lead off to Chester. It could be Horsham in West Sussex with all the third rail around, but Horsham signal box is a rather splendid art deco example.

In Fig. 222 an unidentified class 507 EMU arrives at Hooton from Chester, bound for the Birkenhead direction. The road is set on the adjacent platform for the Helsby line with the 'feather' on the colour light signal.

Fig. 223 shows a class 508, 508 122, departing for Helsby on the left of the two sets of tracks. The moment the first part of the train passes the signal post, the aspect changes to red.

Fig. 224 is still looking towards the double junction. There are only platforms 1, 2 and 3 numbered, although the platform where the station building is has slabs and line edging. Platform 2 is host to class 507 no. 507 027, bound for Chester.

The DMUs for the Chester line used this side of the station, and the Chester line was electrified in 1993. There were originally seven platforms at Hooton, which had GWR expresses from

Fig. 223   Hooton station with EMU departing towards Helsby, January 2015.

Fig. 224   Hooton station overview, February 2015.

Fig. 225   Canning Street North signal box, February 2008.

Fig. 226   Rendel Street crossing, February 2008.

Paddington to Birkenhead, some with sleeping cars, stopping here. There do not appear to be any LNWR structures at Hooton now but the Birkenhead Joint Railway station building is a brick-built gem and quite different from red sandstone neighbours at Ellesmere Port and Helsby.

Hooton station is 8 miles 8 chains (13km) from Chester.

Canning Street North

Date Built	1900
LNWR Type or Builder	LNWR Type 4
No. of Levers	18
Ways of Working	AB
Current Status	Closed and derelict
Listed (Y/N)	N

Birkenhead, together with its rival across the River Mersey, Liverpool, was synonymous with shipping and docks, except that Birkenhead also has a prominent shipbuilder in Cammell Laird. They still repair ships today. Some of the docks were given over to a Royal Navy Museum, and Bidston Dock used to see the import of iron ore for the John Summers steelworks at Shotton, just at the end of the Wirral peninsula but actually in north Wales.

The line that Canning Street North is on is a docks branch to Bidston.

Canning Street North signal box (Fig. 225) survived two world wars but is undergoing its toughest test yet after at least two arson attacks. The box is officially classified as out of use, so could theoretically be brought back into service.

Fig. 226 shows some infrastructure other than double track remains. Pictured is the Rendel Street crossing with what had been a footbridge for pedestrians to bypass the crossing. Note the original massive cast iron gate post for the heavy wooden gates. Shortly after this crossing, the lines belong to the Mersey Docks and Harbour Company, who are now owned by Peel Holdings. There have been initial moves to bring rail freight back to the docks but nothing concrete has happened yet.

Canning Street North signal box is 15 miles and 29 chains (24.7km) from Chester.

Widnes to Warrington

Widnes is another of those unsung places where the country's manufacturing money was made. Speaking of song, though, the celebrated singer-songwriter Paul Simon wrote the song 'Homeward Bound' after he had played at a gig in Widnes and was reputed to have written it at Widnes railway station.

On the railway front, Widnes had a number of chemical works as well as mining nearby to generate traffic and it had its own engine shed, coded 8D. There is even an 8D Association, which has a wealth of information about the railways of Widnes on its website. There were at least seven signal boxes in Widnes, but our journey starts at Carterhouse Junction, some little way out of the town.

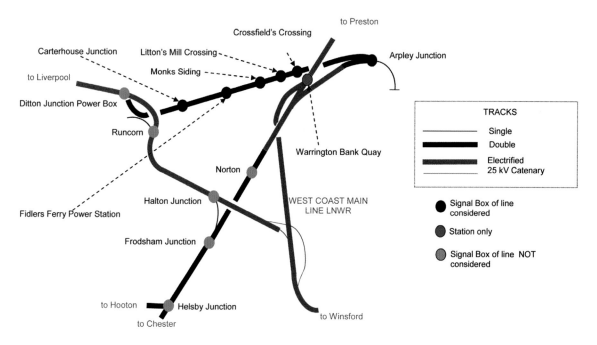

Fig. 227   Widnes–Warrington line schematic diagram.

As for Warrington, the town has always been strategically located between Manchester and Liverpool as well as on the West Coast Main Line and Manchester Ship Canal. As to its industry, the 1936 film *Night Mail* referred to 'the steelworks of Warrington' as the train was flashing past. As we shall see, it also had textile mills and chemical works. Much coal traffic is generated by Fiddlers Ferry power station.

Please note that the punctuation used here follows that used by the railway. Also, although Fidlers Ferry is popularly spelt Fiddlers Ferry on most maps, the former is the railway spelling, which is usually the spelling that appeared on the act of parliament for that piece of railway construction.

Station names in the Welsh language often suffered at the hands of clerks drafting parliamentary bills.

Carterhouse Junction

Date Built	1896
LNWR Type or Builder	LNWR Type 4
No. of Levers	30
Ways of Working	AB
Current Status	Demolished April 2007
Listed (Y/N)	N

Fig. 228   Carterhouse Junction signal box, October 2005.

Fig. 229 Carterhouse Junction with signals and Sankey Canal towards Fiddlers Ferry, October 2005.

Carterhouse Junction was a junction of just one running line down to Widnes docks and there were two private sidings. After the docks branch closed, the main siding – so called – was used by Tarmac, and there were other sidings for Astra Zeneca Chemicals and LaFarge tarmac.

The box in Fig. 228 has been switched out for some time and is slowly slipping into the Sankey (or St Helens) Canal behind it. The scaffolding and wood bearers at the rear were put in to arrest the slippage. The box had already been the subject of an arson attack and was to suffer yet again before being demolished. Behind the Sankey Canal is the River Mersey.

In Fig. 229 the signals of Carterhouse Junction signal box bear testimony to its lack of use – they are all off and the box is switched out.

The bracket signal has had its subsidiary arm for the main siding (what was the docks branch) removed, as the siding is no longer there. Note how the steady post for the bracket signal guy wires spans four tracks.

The sidings in view are described on the signalling diagram as 'Sullivan Works' but were in later years Astra Zeneca's. One of Fiddlers Ferry power station's eight cooling towers is in the background. The Sankey Canal fishers have the right weather for it.

Carterhouse Junction signal box used to be 16 miles and 27 chains (26.3km) from the former Timperley Junction. Timperley Junction no longer exists, but the mileage simply fixes the box at a point along the track. The alternative would be to change all the quarter-mile posts, of which there must be tens of thousands.

Fidlers Ferry (S)

Date Built	1967
LNWR Type or Builder	BR London Midland Region Type 15
No. of Levers	45
Ways of Working	AB
Current Status	Active
Listed (Y/N)	N

Fidlers Ferry power station signal box is another BR standard box that might just have seen steam engines working past it, as loco sheds in Warrington and Speke Junction Liverpool did not close until 1968.

The box resembles Ellesmere Port, and the Type 15 seems to have been the most popular of the BR structures. The box does not have any point rodding coming out of it, and all points controlled by the box appear to be electrically operated. All home

Fig. 230 Fidlers Ferry signal box, February 2015.

Fig. 231   Fidlers Ferry outer home signal, February 2015.

Fig. 232   Fidlers Ferry bracket and ground disc signals, February 2015.

signals appear to be semaphores, though. There is a crossover for down trains from Warrington to access the power station and there are three loops within the power station that handle loaded trains and disposal of the unloaded ones. There are two more sidings: one for flyash, which is the product of burning the coal, and another for crippled wagons. Only the lead point off to the two sidings is switched from the box, the other is manually switched with a local lever.

The box is in good condition in Fig. 230, and this is an example where the box is so busy it cannot be allowed to deteriorate.

As all power station traffic is to and from Warrington Arpley Junction, the survey concentrates on that piece of the line. The signal depicted in Fig. 231 is the down outer home and is motor worked – the motor is visible towards the foot of the post. The Sankey Canal is in the foreground and is home to all sorts of vessels.

Fig. 232 shows the approach to the power station from the down, left-hand, direction. The bracket signal subsidiary arm signals a train from the down main, across the crossover in front of the box and into the power station. The subsidiary arm is qualified by the route indicator, which can show any one of four letters to indicate which of the three loops or siding group the train is to take after it has left the up main line and crossed into the power station complex. The ground disc on the far side of the tracks has the same four different routes ascribed, and this signal is for reversing moves off the up main, or right-hand side, tracks into the power station.

Fig. 233 gives an indication of what it takes to keep the nation's lights on. A Freightliner class 70, 70 006, with a loaded coal train, takes the crossover and point into the power station. The route indicator will have either A or B indicated for the coal hopper approach tracks, while B and C are where

Fig. 233   Fidlers Ferry bracket signal; a class 70 arrives with a coal train, February 2015.

Fig. 234 The class 70 and coal train head for the unloading bay at Fiddlers Ferry, February 2015.

Fig. 235 A class 60 and coal empties depart Fidlers Ferry for Warrington and beyond, February 2015.

the unloaded trains can end up. Note that there is a 15mph speed limit over the crossover into the yard and that the crossover, which is right in front of the box, is electrically operated. The grey box by the speed restriction sign is a point motor.

The ground disc we saw in Fig. 232 is on the left, with its four caption or stencil boxes beneath it.

In Fig. 234 the class 70 and train make their way to the unloading hoppers, and the signaller at Fidlers Ferry signal box is able to give Train out of Section to Monks Siding signal box, as the tail lamp is visible. The tail lamp confirms that the train has not divided in the section. There are

two BR 'domino' absolute block instruments in the box.

No sooner has the class 70 gone round to the unloading area than DB Schenker class 60, 60 044, with a train of EWS-branded empty hoppers, is given the road for Arpley Junction (Fig. 235). The locomotive and train are on track C, with track A to the left and track B and the two sidings to the right. The signal on the far left is to guard the main up running line towards Warrington Arpley Junction.

Fig. 236 gives another collateral view of the box as the class 60 and train head off for Arpley Junction.

Fig. 236 (left) The class 60 and coal empties regain the main line at Fidlers Ferry, February 2015.

Fig. 237 (below) A class 66 moves onto the main line at Fidlers Ferry to back down onto its train, February 2015.

Fig. 238   Class 66 signalled into loop C at Fidlers Ferry, February 2015.

Fig. 239   The class 66 waits to leave loop C with its train, February 2015.

Although the loops are return loops in the sense that if the train keeps going it will reverse its direction, there is also a requirement to run round a train when it comes to flyash hoppers. The EWS-branded class 66, 66 089, heads along the up main for a short way in Fig. 237 before reversing back down into the power station yard.

Fig. 238 shows the class 66 reversing along the up main back into the yard. Note the track-circuited ground disc stencil box is showing C for the middle loop of the three. The entire layout is track circuited except for the two sidings. The signals here all have the box GSM-R phone number.

In Fig. 239 the class 66 is now coupled up to the flyash wagons and awaits a departure path to Arpley Junction.

Fidlers Ferry signal box is 14 miles and 46 chains (23.5km) from the former Timperley Junction.

In recent years the mechanical signalling was removed after Fidlers Ferry although the boxes remain for the present; as a result, a mixture of older photographs depicting an earlier era is used here, together with more modern photographs where appropriate. The way of working described may also not be what it is now.

Monks Siding

Date Built	1875
LNWR Type or Builder	LNWR Type 3+
No. of Levers	20
Ways of Working	TCB, AB
Current Status	Active
Listed (Y/N)	Y

Fig. 240   Monks Siding signal box, February 2015.

Fig. 241 *Monks Siding signal box and the view towards Fidlers Ferry, October 2005.*

Moving on to the outskirts of Warrington, this box, apart from being a block post, was established to control entry to a wireworks. The works has long since disappeared and the site behind the box is occupied by modern housing. In 2012 the box was updated with a panel to work AB to Fidlers Ferry but TCB to Arpley Junction.

Fig. 240 shows one of the oldest boxes on the network with what looks like the original name board without punctuation. It reflects an age where the tradespeople engaged in making the mould for the cast iron board would have had a minimal education and almost certainly have left school at fourteen, as was then the norm, if indeed school had been attended at all.

Fig. 242 *Monks Siding and the view towards Litton's Mill Crossing, October 2005.*

The box is a bit too close to the track for modern sensibilities – hence the red-and-white-chequered limited clearance signs.

Fig. 241 is a view looking back towards Fidlers Ferry, rewound ten years, and now the signal boxes are so close together that the distant signals are fixed. The reason for these boxes being so close is that there are crossings associated with factories from now on.

The trailing crossover would have been required for trains from either line to access the wireworks behind the box.

Fig. 242 is looking the other way towards Warrington Arpley Junction. Litton's Mill Crossing is only 25 chains or 450m from Monks Siding and so the home and not-so-distant signal up the line are the next box's signals. Note that the home signal for the Fidlers Ferry direction, which is on a bracket, has a further 'doll' on the bracket for the now removed siding.

Monks Siding signal box is 11 miles and 70 chains (19.1km) from the former Timperley Junction.

Litton's Mill Crossing

Date Built	1890
LNWR Type or Builder	LNWR Type 4
No. of Levers	18
Ways of Working	Gate
Current Status	Active
Listed (Y/N)	N

Fig. 243 shows the box looking a bit shabby but mostly original. Here there are manually operated gates. The black rod going vertically down between the gate post and the gate is the locking mechanism from the box, which is interlocked with the signals. If the box is switched out and the gates are left across the tracks, a key is issued to train crews to open the gates, drive their train through and then relock.

Fig. 244 shows the view back to Monks Siding and Widnes. The signal in the picture on the right is the same signal we saw at Monks Siding but the distant is obscured by the vegetation. The distant

Fig. 243   Litton's Mill Crossing signal box, October 2005.

Fig. 244   Litton's Mill Crossing signal box looking towards Monks Siding, October 2005.

signals are all fixed at caution, thus preparing trains to expect the next signal to be at danger.

The blue buildings visible in Fig. 245 are Crosfield's factory, now owned by Lever Brothers. The lamp on the gate is a former oil lamp, converted to run off electricity. When the gates are across the road the lamp still shines towards road users as there is a lens on both sides of the lamp.

Litton's Mill Crossing signal box is 11 miles and 45 chains (18.6km) from the former Timperley Junction.

Crosfields Crossing

Date Built	1906
LNWR Type or Builder	LNWR Type 4
No. of Levers	18
Ways of Working	AB
Current Status	Closed – houses relays
Listed (Y/N)	N

Fig. 246 shows Crosfields Crossing signal box in some sort of time warp, hidden away inside the factory premises. Very little has changed in 100

Fig. 245   Litton's Mill Crossing signal box looking towards Crosfields Crossing, October 2005.

Fig. 246   Crosfields Crossing signal box, October 2005.

Fig. 247   Crosfields Crossing home and distant signals, October 2005.

Fig. 248   Arpley Junction signal box, February 2015.

years apart from the steps. The box was to be refurbished in 2007, but although it is still in position the signallers are not, as it is now a relay room for interlocking equipment for the replacement signalling. It is only 10 chains (180m) from Litton's Mill Crossing signal box.

The home and distant signal together, shown in Fig. 247, are the same signal we saw at Litton's Mill Crossing by the big cylindrical tanks.

Crosfields Crossing signal box is 11 miles and 35 chains (18.4km) from the former Timperley Junction.

Arpley Junction (AJ)

Date Built	1918
LNWR Type or Builder	LNWR Type 5
No. of Levers	54
Ways of Working	TCB
Current Status	Active
Listed (Y/N)	N

Arpley is a district of Warrington, and the box was close to Arpley station and engine shed, a sub-shed of Warrington Dallam, now no longer there. The box is also close to Warrington Bank Quay station on the West Coast Main Line.

The scene in Fig. 248 is after the changes to the signalling in 2012. The box works TCB to Monks Siding, and axle counters are used to simulate a signaller observing the tail lamp and giving Train out of Section. The box also works TCB to Warrington power box. There is still a good deal of point rodding coming out of the box, and also some retro gardening, with the pampas grass.

Fig. 249 shows the view from the Slutcher's Lane overbridge back towards the blue premises of Lever Brothers, or Crosfield's, as it once was. The off-white band running horizontally across the top half of the picture is Warrington Bank Quay station canopy, and some of the 25kV catenary support masts can be seen. In the foreground is a limit of shunt marker.

Fig. 250 is Arpley Junction with the box in attendance. The view is from other side of the Slutcher's Lane overbridge.

The tracks from Crosfields Crossing and Widnes come in from the left. The chord to the West Coast Main Line departs and curves round to the right.

The interchange sidings have not been used for some years but most recently they were used to stable crippled wagons. On the first rusty point into the yard there is a trap point halfway along the point straight switch rail. Clearly this is a space-saving

Fig. 249   Arpley Junction looking towards Crosfields Crossing, February 2015.

wheeze, as there is no space for a conventional trap point before the running line junction point.

Another point to note is that there is a switched diamond crossing at the junction, and the switches appear to have facing-point locks. Also on view is the collection of old yard lamps, now defunct.

In Fig. 251 the camera has moved back to the first side of the overbridge but this time is looking along at the chord to the West Coast Main Line. The point work in the foreground is more conventional, with a trap point and static diamond crossing in the foreground. Note that there is a triple-decker ground disc signal by the trap point, so some mechanical signalling survives. The yard houses a motley collection of wagons and a class 66 is also lurking in there. The two tracks curving to the WCML actually meet up with the line to Runcorn East and Helsby Junction but there are crossovers to get onto the WCML proper.

Arpley Junction signal box is 11 miles and 3 chains (17.8km) from the former Timperley Junction.

Manchester Area

Manchester was one on the major centres of LNWR signalling, as it was for several other companies, notably the Lancashire and Yorkshire Railway. The ex-LNWR lines are the most prominent and it is understandable that much of the infrastructure was an early candidate for modernization as the main lines around Manchester had been electrified with the 25kV system in the 1960s.

Fig. 250   Arpley Junction, February 2015.

Fig. 251   Arpley Junction looking towards the WCML, February 2015.

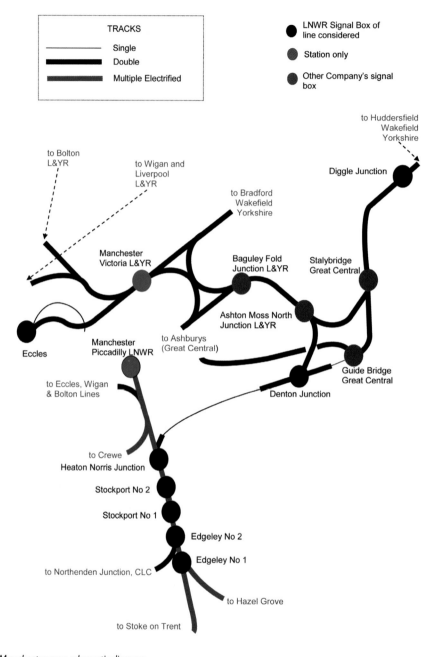

Fig. 252 Manchester area schematic diagram.

The situation now is that hardly any mechanical LNWR line signalling survives, but some boxes work track circuit block, mostly under the 25kV electrification wires. The journey starts at Diggle, in the foothills of the Pennines and yet only a few miles from metropolitan Manchester.

Diggle Junction (DE)

Date Built	1885
LNWR Type or Builder	LNWR Type 4+
No. of Levers	26
Ways of Working	TCB
Current Status	Active
Listed (Y/N)	N

Diggle was originally in the West Riding of Yorkshire but now belongs to Greater Manchester. This is a village that has the rare accolade of a local fish and chip shop that is a listed building. It has become an attractive commuter village and there is pressure to reopen the station, which was closed in 1963.

The village is not far away from Standedge Tunnel, just 3 miles and 66yd (4.9km), which was a notorious bottleneck. By 1894 the tunnel capacity had been increased to four tracks. To match this increase, two further tracks were laid in parallel to the original double-track LNWR main line and one end of the effective loop met at Diggle. The station was increased to four platforms.

Consequently the box was constructed on a large scale, but after reduction down to two tracks and station closure, the box was similarly reduced to twenty-six levers. Fig. 253 is the view from Ward Lane road overbridge.

The box has some mechanical leverage coming out of it as there is a trailing crossover and a down passing loop, where down means towards Huddersfield and up towards Manchester.

Fig. 254 is not a bad view from the office window – Saddleworth Moor. The down passing loop and crossover are also in view. The size of the girder bridge gives the clue that there were four tracks here. The galvanized steel mast to the right is for GSM-R reception. The view is towards Huddersfield.

First TransPennine Express class 185, 185 108, is hurrying up towards Manchester past the box in Fig. 255. Note that there are catch points on the down passing loop.

The line then comes down from the hills towards Manchester and passes through Great Central Railway, later LNER, territory to Denton Junction.

Diggle Junction signal box is 14 miles 59 chains (23.7km) from Manchester Victoria station.

Fig. 253   Diggle Junction signal box, February 2015.

Fig. 254   Diggle Junction signal box looking towards Huddersfield, February 2015.

Fig. 255   Diggle Junction signal box with a class 185 heading for Manchester, February 2015.

Denton Junction (DJ)

Date Built	1888
LNWR Type or Builder	LNWR Type 4+
No. of Levers	18
Ways of Working	TCB, AB
Current Status	Active
Listed (Y/N)	N

Denton prospered as a centre of the felt hat-making industry during a time in the nineteenth century when it was considered unseemly to be seen in public bare-headed. Although the supposed epicentre of the hat business was Stockport, where the hat museum now is, Denton was the place for felts. The last hat factory closed in 1980. In common with many places in these islands, Denton also had coal mines to supply the factories and domestic housing. The town also produced Oldham batteries, which were marketed with the immortal words 'I told 'em Oldham', no doubt in reference to the product's quality and reliability.

Fig. 256 shows the changes that have happened at Denton Junction over the ten years since the first visit. The box has acquired air conditioning and the signaller has acquired a BMW 3 Series Touring E91 as an upgrade from the BMW 3 Series Saloon E46, both in blue. The straight 'main lines' past the box run from Guide Bridge to Heaton Norris Junction and are TCB controlled. The lines are actually a long loop just under 1½ miles (2.4km) long, with single track at both ends.

The lines that curve away from the front of the box by the buffer stops are the double-track, AB, mechanically signalled line to Ashton Moss North Junction, which featured in Volume 1. Paradoxically, the singled loop line sees far more traffic than the double-track main line. The buffer stops are some of the largest and most crudely constructed on the network and now have nothing to stop.

Note the concrete gradient marker on the same side as the stops to the right.

In Fig. 257 some of Denton Junction's remaining semaphore signals on the line to Ashton are concealing themselves in the undergrowth, as well they might. The box is a few hundred yards to the right and the distant signal is fixed at caution with no green lens fitted or mechanicals to move it.

The class 66, 66 507, runs light engine from right to left past the box in Fig. 258. The loco is headed to Guide Bridge depot to take up track-maintenance duties.

Fig. 259 is the view from the Stamford Road overbridge. The Ashton branch heads off to the right opposite the box. Meanwhile a class 66, 66 564, is on a rubbish train, known as the 'bin liner'. The wagons are branded Viridor, a recycling company. The class 66 and train had been held at the grey colour light signal with the feather, beyond the last wagon, for twenty minutes waiting for the road onto the single-line section towards Guide Bridge.

There is now a short detour to Eccles before we rejoin the main line from Manchester Piccadilly.

Fig. 256   Denton Junction signal box, February 2015.

Fig. 257   Denton Junction semaphore signals, February 2015.

Fig. 258   Denton Junction with a class 66 running light to Guide Bridge, February 2015.

Eccles (ES)

Date Built	1933
LNWR Type or Builder	LMS Type 11b
No. of Levers	Nx panel
Ways of Working	TCB, OTW
Current Status	Active
Listed (Y/N)	N

Eccles is famous for Eccles cakes and featured on one of Michael Portillo's *Great Railway Journey* TV programmes with the ever-adaptable presenter involved in the baking process. Eccles is on the LNWR line from Manchester to Liverpool. The line is referred to as 'Chat Moss', which is a large expanse of peat bog. George Stephenson, the line's engineer, famously spent some months establishing first wooden foundations and then brushwood to provide a bed for the railway to float on, which it still does today.

Fig. 259   Denton Junction and a class 66 running to Guide Bridge with a waste train, February 2015.

Fig. 260   Eccles signal box, February 2015.

Fig. 261 *Eccles looking towards Manchester Victoria, February 2015.*

The station had been built in 1830, making it a very early, pre-Victorian destination on the line with a string of railway firsts making it the forerunner of modern railway passenger lines in the world.

The trains now run from Manchester Victoria, which was originally L&YR. The line had originally been quadruple track and the layout partially reflects that. The line was electrified in 2015 as part of the Liverpool–Manchester 25kV scheme.

The box in Fig. 260 has survived another bout of modernization. In front of the box is a facing crossover to permit access to the goods loop on the up, or Manchester-bound, side. From the end of the goods loop is a line to LaFarge cement terminal, which is located alongside the Manchester Ship Canal at Salford Quays. The box supervises one train working to the MSC.

In Fig. 261 the view is towards Manchester Victoria as a First TransPennine Express class 185, 185 117, hurries to that destination. Note the single-track branch line to the LaFarge terminal on the left, which proceeds in the same direction as the train before diving under the main line. Note the box obscured on the right, opposite the signaller's red car.

Eccles signal box was involved in an accident in 1984. A passenger train headed by a class 45 diesel loco was on its way from Liverpool to Scarborough and was given Train out of Section from Astley signal box, the next one to Eccles, and the line was worked AB at the time. From there on there was no AWS. Track workers were at work and this was allegedly causing intermittent track circuit indications in Eccles box. Two semaphore signals were passed at danger and this was thought to be because of bad sighting due to construction of a new road and buildings near the line side. The passenger train ran into the back of a slow-moving oil tanker train. The passenger train driver lost his life as did two passengers.

The cause was attributed to the driver passing two signals at danger and there being no AWS to audibly warn him; the signal sighting was a contributory factor. AWS was provided and sighting white paint applied to those structures that confused the aspect. No fault could be found with the track circuits.

Eccles signal box is 27 miles 59 chains (44.6km) from Liverpool Lime Street station.

We now head back to the LNWR main line at Heaton Norris Junction.

Heaton Norris Junction (HN)

Date Built	1955
LNWR Type or Builder	BR London Midland Region Type 14
No. of Levers	125
Ways of Working	TCB, AB
Current Status	Active
Listed (Y/N)	N

Fig. 262 *Heaton Norris Junction signal box, February 2015.*

Fig. 263   Heaton Norris Junction goods warehouse, August 2006.

Now we have reached suburban Stockport, and while Stockport historically was in Cheshire, Heaton Norris was in Lancashire. Heaton Norris Rovers football team were renamed Stockport County FC in 1883. The iconic Stockport viaduct over the M60 motorway and River Mersey was an early construction in 1840 and used 11 million bricks – it is one of the world's largest brick-built structures and is Grade II listed. It carries the LNWR main line from Manchester to the south.

No such architectural accolade as listing has yet befallen Heaton Norris Junction signal box (Fig. 262). Heaton Norris Junction works TCB to Manchester Piccadilly signalling centre and AB to Stockport No. 2.

While there isn't much of the present railway territory that shouts LNWR, across the track is the former goods warehouse that does (Fig. 263).

There are four main running lines past the box; the junction to Guide Bridge is double track but quickly goes to single. The fifth, non-electrified track at the far side of the picture is described as a loco-holding siding off the up goods loop on the Guide Bridge branch.

Heaton Norris Junction signal box is 183 miles 63 chains (295.8km) from London Euston.

Stockport No. 2 (ST2)

Date Built	1890
LNWR Type or Builder	LNWR Type 4+
No. of Levers	90
Ways of Working	AB
Current Status	Active
Listed (Y/N)	N

All the boxes at Stockport and Edgeley, a little to the south, were to have been closed when the Italian Ansaldo 'off the shelf' system was to be commissioned by 2004. In the event the project encountered major problems and the boxes are still controlling part of one of Network Rail's flagship routes. The

Fig. 264   Stockport No. 2 signal box, April 2013.

Fig. 265   Stockport station looking towards Heaton Norris Junction, April 2013.

Fig. 266   Stockport No. 1 signal box, April 2013.

equipment outside the box is twenty-first century and that inside mostly nineteenth.

Although there is no mechanical signalling here, the crash of levers in a frame as the box is being worked is a familiar sound, as is the remorseless tingling of block bells. The box in Fig. 264 has been reduced in lever count from 120 so was on a par with Crewe Junction at Shrewsbury.

In Fig. 265 the camera has swung round somewhat less than 90 degrees to focus on Stockport Viaduct, mentioned under Heaton Norris Junction above. The quadruple tracks head off for Heaton Norris Junction and Manchester Piccadilly. The down slow is limited to 75mph (120km/h) and the fast 90mph (145km/h). The signals appear to be at the same distances although the usual policy is to allow greater distances between signals the faster the permitted line speed, but at this location sections are short. Stockport Viaduct is 579yd (530m) long with twenty-seven spans.

The box supervises nine carriage sidings in addition to its main line duties.

There was a legend that all trains that crossed over Stockport Viaduct had to stop at Stockport station and that this was embedded in the Manchester and Birmingham Railway Act of 1837. This was rather like all GWR passenger trains having to stop at Swindon refreshment room until they were bought out. Later scrutiny of the act revealed this to be a myth.

Stockport No. 2 signal box is 183 miles 8 chains (294.7km) from Euston station.

Stockport No. 1 (ST1)

Date Built	1884
LNWR Type or Builder	LNWR Type 4+
No. of Levers	98
Ways of Working	AB
Current Status	Active
Listed (Y/N)	N

At the other, southern, end of Stockport station is Stockport No. 1 signal box (Fig. 267), which is tucked into the platform 3, 3A, 4 island. Platform 4

Fig. 267   Stockport station looking towards No. 2 box, April 2013.

Fig. 268 Edgeley Junction No. 2 signal box, April 2013.

Fig. 269 Edgeley Junction No. 2 signal box, rear view and running lines, April 2013.

can only handle eleven coaches as a result, whereas platform 3 is fourteen coach lengths. The only other place on the network where there are two signal boxes of such a size so close to one another is Shrewsbury. Note how the larger LNWR signal boxes all have the galvanized steel hooped fire escape, whether they have the internal staircase or not.

Fig. 267 is the view from opposite No. 1 signal box towards Manchester Piccadilly; No. 2 is in the distance near the end of the platform that the camera is on. The canopies are modern but the station buildings are LNWR and retain much of their character.

Stockport No. 1 signal box is 182 miles 73 chains (294.4km) from London Euston.

Edgeley Junction No. 2 (EJ2)

Date Built	1884
LNWR Type or Builder	LNWR Type 4+
No. of Levers	54
Ways of Working	AB
Current Status	Active
Listed (Y/N)	N

Edgeley is a district in the south of Stockport. There was a steam depot at Stockport Edgeley until 1968, and it was from this depot that driver John Axon GC set off on that fateful day in February 1957

– *see* the section on Chapel-en-le-Frith, above. He was returning to Stockport from Buxton when the incident occurred and was due to attend Stockport County's home game that afternoon.

Edgeley is also the site of two junctions and the reason for the next two signal boxes.

Fig. 268 shows the box is hemmed in by track. The track at the rear of the box is the line to Northenden Junction, which has a signal box that is of Cheshire Lines Committee (CLC) origin. The conglomeration of railways in Lancashire and Cheshire required much joint line working and the CLC was an alliance of the Midland, Great Northern and Great Central railways. The last two in the list were eventually to form part of the LNER so CLC lines and signalling will appear in one of the LNER books. These two tracks become single track within a mile but are joined by a line from New Mills South Junction, which provides the Midland Railway component and is covered in Volume 1.

Fig. 269 gives a clearer view of the junction arrangements at Edgeley Junction No. 2 and of the admin block on the back of the box. There are a total of three AWS yellow ramps just in view. These provide an audible warning of the signal status, and in exceptional conditions will apply the train's brakes automatically unless the train driver overrides it. There are two warnings – one for line clear and one for caution – so even if the driver has not

Fig. 270   Edgeley Junction No. 1 signal box, February 2015.

Fig. 271   Edgeley Junction No. 1 signal box, rear view and running lines, July 2005.

actually observed a signal's aspect there is a sound to indicate what the status was.

Stockport Edgeley Junction No. 2 signal box is 182 miles 53 chains (294km) from London Euston.

Edgeley Junction No. 1 (EJ1)

Date Built	1884
LNWR Type or Builder	LNWR Type 4+
No. of Levers	54
Ways of Working	AB
Current Status	Active
Listed (Y/N)	N

Edgeley Junction No. 1 signal box is shown in Fig. 270. The lines to Northenden Junction that have passed No. 2 box curve away behind the box. The Hazel Grove junction is the junction from where all the mileages for the Buxton branch were calculated; the point for part of the junction is to the left of the figure. The box has been reduced in lever count from ninety when built to fifty-four now. There were originally eight lines running in front of the box.

Fig. 271 shows No. 1 signal box from the Northenden Junction side, and there is a track renewals storage site in the V of the junction. The box is only 17 chains or 310m from the No. 2 box. The absolute block working was retained initially because the signals and junctions are so close together: TCB would require them all to be interlocked in turn or slotted before a train could be passed.

Stockport Edgeley Junction No. 1 signal box is 182 miles 36 chains (293.6km) from London Euston.

Liverpool Area

The simplified schematic diagram in Fig. 272 shows a system that is a shadow of its former self but is nevertheless indicative of how much rail traffic there had been. The LNWR inherited the prestige passenger route into Lime Street from railway's earliest networked railway beginnings with the Liverpool and Manchester Railway in 1830. The LNWR vied with the L&YR for a superior presence at the docks. Liverpool had been a port of some significance since the eighteenth century and developed into the Cunard Transatlantic Liner terminal. The city has more Georgian buildings than any outside London. At one time it contributed more to the exchequer than any other place, including London. The waterfront in Liverpool is a designated world heritage site and the arts and medicine are also prominent in the city's achievements.

Our journey begins after Chat Moss at the next signal box on from Eccles, where we left off. As with the Manchester area, there is hardly any AB working left and after further electrification there will be none at all.

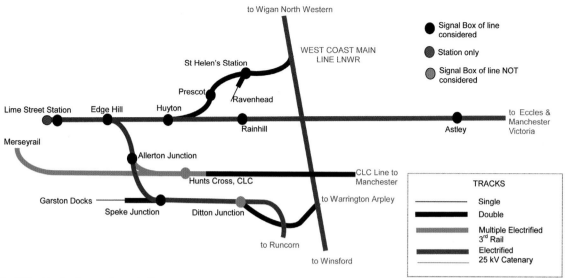

Fig. 272   Liverpool area schematic diagram.

Astley (AY)

Date Built	1972
LNWR Type or Builder	BR London Midland Region Type 15
No. of Levers	15
Ways of Working	TCB
Current Status	Active
Listed (Y/N)	N

Astley as a community became established in the nineteenth century and developed into a mining community once the railway provided a means of getting the coal to market. There was a textile mill here too. Now it is a commuter village as it is roughly halfway between Liverpool and Manchester. The last coal was transported out in the 1970s and the station had already closed by 1956.

Fig. 273 shows not only the box but the fairly unusual crossing arrangements, where there were user-worked gates at the time of the survey. No doubt the signaller retains control over the gate locking and this will be interlocked with signals. The gates appear to offer access to a farm track. The box housing the gate lock by the right-hand gate post looks to be lever worked.

In Fig. 274 Coradia class 175, 175 106, is scampering across Chat Moss and the crossing towards

Fig. 274   A class 175 hurries from Manchester past Astley crossing, July 2007.

Fig. 273   Astley signal box, July 2007.

Fig. 275   Rainhill signal box, November 2014.

Fig. 276   Historic Rainhill station, December 2005.

Liverpool. In the early to mid-1960s, the passenger trains on this route were still steam hauled, usually by ex-LMS Black Five 4–6–0 locos, and some stirring runs were had on the largely billiard table flatness hereabouts.

Astley signal box is 22 miles 54 chains (36.5km) from Liverpool Lime Street station.

The railway crosses Earlestown Junction, where north–south and east–west railways meet.

Rainhill

Date Built	1896
LNWR Type or Builder	LNWR Type 4
No. of Levers	25
Ways of Working	TCB
Current Status	Closed 2007
Listed (Y/N)	N

Rainhill is for ever enshrined in railway history for the Rainhill Trials, which decided the winner of the various steam locomotive technologies there were in 1829. Stephenson's *Rocket* was the winner and most subsequent steam locomotives can trace their lineage back that far. It effectively turned Britain into an industrialized nation from a largely agrarian one. The one event to mar the Trials was the death of MP William Huskisson, who was run over by the *Rocket*. There is a listed memorial structure to William Huskisson on the line side near Newton-le-Willows.

In Fig. 275 the box had already been closed for some years and doesn't look to have a future under the wires.

Fig. 276 shows Rainhill station, plodding on towards its 200th anniversary, which it should achieve as a Grade II listed building. The footbridge and signal box beyond complete the scene.

Rainhill signal box is 9 miles 4 chains (14.6km) from Liverpool Lime Street station.

Huyton (HN)

Date Built	1899
LNWR Type or Builder	LNWR Type 4+
No. of Levers	36
Ways of Working	TCB, AB
Current Status	Demolished 2014
Listed (Y/N)	N

Huyton is part of the Liverpool area and was a coal mining area until the 1980s. The district has strong associations with footballers and the Beatles. It was also the constituency of Labour Prime Minister Harold Wilson.

The station originally had four platforms to service the junction for St Helen's as well as the Chat Moss line. That layout is being reintroduced as part of the electrification of the Liverpool–Manchester line, which meant the box was in the way and consequently demolished.

Fig. 277 shows the box in 2005. The surviving ground disc is for a reversing move over the trailing crossover just to the left of the box out of shot. The box worked TCB to Warrington and Edge Hill and AB to Prescot on the St Helen's line. The view is towards Liverpool Lime Street.

Fig. 278 is the view towards Manchester. The feather on the colour light signal is for the branch to St Helen's and Wigan North Western, about ¼ mile (400m) from the station. The original 1830 station at Huyton was Huyton Quarry, which closed in 1938 and was demolished.

The journey now deviates up the branch to cover Prescot and St Helen's.

Prescot (PT)

Date Built	1954
LNWR Type or Builder	LNWR Type 5
No. of Levers	36
Ways of Working	AB
Current Status	Demolished 2012
Listed (Y/N)	N

Prescot had an active clock-making industry and the town's museum celebrates that. As at Helsby, the town had a large factory for cable making under the BICC or British Insulated Callender's Cables banner. Some of the larger drums of mains power cable were so big that Weltrol or 45-ton bogie well wagons were needed for their transport.

The estate of the Earls of Derby is nearby, and an offshoot of that is Knowsley Safari Park.

The signal box was an amalgamation of LNWR parts and London Midland Region components.

Fig. 279 shows Prescot signal box together with the small bracketed-out starter for the St Helens direction. The signal is sighted to clear the station canopy just behind the camera.

Fig. 277   Huyton signal box, December 2005.

Fig. 278   Huyton station, December 2005.

Fig. 279   Prescot signal box, December 2005.

Fig. 280   Prescot signal box and station looking towards St Helens, December 2005.

St Helens Station (SH)

Date Built	1891
LNWR Type or Builder	LNWR Type 4+
No. of Levers	24, IFS panel
Ways of Working	AB, TCB, OTS
Current Status	Active
Listed (Y/N)	N

Fig. 280 is still looking towards St Helens but here the section signal is visible past the road over-bridge, with the help of the sighting board. The up, towards St Helens, siding on the left was used for goods trains but the connection has been plain lined. The yellow quarter mile marker near the siding pronounces 1 mile and 60 chains (2.8km) from a point just after Huyton Junction.

Fig. 281 is the view from the other side of the footbridge towards Huyton. Class 150, 150 228, is coasting to a stop at the up platform with a train for St Helen's. The station is reasonably busy, with about half a million passengers per year, and is set to get busier.

Prescot station is 1 mile 53 chains (2.7km) from the point near Huyton Junction.

St Helens is most famous for the manufacture of glass by the Pilkington firm, who are still active in the town. In common with other towns nearby, coal mining was also a staple in the economic diet. Other industries included brewing and ethical drugs and the Ravenhead glass works, subsequently bought out by Belgian company Durobor.

As well as railways developing the town rapidly in the mid-nineteenth century, the St Helens, or Sankey, Canal played its part. We have already seen the other end of the Sankey Canal near Fiddlers Ferry power station (*see* Figs 228 and 229).

St Helens station signal box is shown in Fig. 282. Although the beginning of the electrification masts is there, the box has so far been spared the wire mesh grilles that go with that operation. The mineral sidings, only one of which is now in use, are in front of the box and there are several others behind the box obscured by the inevitable birch trees. The box supervises the working of the Ravenhead single-line branch, which leaves the main running line right after the up platform in the Wigan direction. This branch is worked one train

Fig. 281   Prescot station looking towards Huyton, December 2005.

Fig. 282   St Helens signal box, November 2014.

Fig. 283   St Helens signal box and station, November 2014.

Fig. 284   St Helens station and junction, November 2014.

staff, where a token is issued to the train crew that, as well as being authority to proceed, is the literal key to unlock and relock points on the branch. The train's singular presence is secured by track circuits. The signal box is provided with an individual function switch panel to work the Ravenhead branch.

In addition to this, there is a further branch from the main line for Pilkington's Oil Terminal, which is half a mile (800m) from the station and is ground frame worked by the train crew but unlocked by the box.

Fig. 283 shows that some mechanical signalling survives: not only is there a ground disc by the box to let a goods train out onto the up running line, but there is a pair of discs to signal a reversing move over the trailing crossover or into the siding by the box. Note the redundant signal wire pulleys that are fastened to the platform face.

The ultra-bright LED SH 3 signal looks as though it could use a spirit level but perhaps it was put this way for sighting purposes. Sixty-year-old wooden post bracket signals might lean over a bit, but they had an excuse. The view is towards Wigan North Western station.

In Fig. 284 the cupboard is even more bare of mechanical signalling looking towards Huyton. The two tracks leading off to the left are the Ravenhead branch, which becomes single line within about half a mile. The station building is completely new, and made, not surprisingly, mostly of glass.

This seems to work as a structure, and is a definite improvement, in terms of passenger comfort, on what went before.

St Helens station is 5 miles 16 chains (8.4km) from the point near Huyton Junction and 7 miles 20 chains (11.7km) from Wigan Springs Branch junction.

Edge Hill (LE)

Date Built	1961
LNWR Type or Builder	BR London Midland Region Powerbox
No. of Levers	Nx panel
Ways of Working	TCB
Current Status	Active
Listed (Y/N)	N

Power boxes have not been covered so far, but Edge Hill is pivotal to operations in Liverpool. The original station is a very early Liverpool and Manchester Railway example and is not open to the public. Its successor is still worthy of note. There had been a massive goods yard here as well as a connection to Wapping Docks. Edge Hill was also home to the LNWR's main passenger engine sheds, coded 8A under BR, which housed Duchess and Princess Pacific locomotives.

In Fig. 285 Edge Hill signal box is trying hard to look modern but the 1950s/60s 'Edge Hill 400 Yards' London Midland Region sign, pointing to the right,

Fig. 285   Edge Hill signal box, February 2015.

2. The pair of tracks where the DMU is and immediately to its right are the Chat Moss lines to Huyton and beyond. The DMU is a class 156, 156 428, and the cab caption looks like Manchester Airport. This fits in, as Northern Rail do run such a service. There is also a service to Liverpool South Parkway (formerly Allerton) for Liverpool John Lennon Airport.
3. The two lines next to them are the main line to Ditton Junction and Runcorn, Crewe and Euston.
4. The lines outside the box are various engineer's and carriage sidings although not populated as such.

does not enhance that. The steam age water tower on the right is an LNWR product and reminiscent of the one we saw at Holyhead. These structures are so massive that it is presumably cheaper to leave them standing than knock them down. In any case it's looking to have a roof garden soon.

Fig. 286 is the view is from the Picton Road overbridge looking towards Lime Street station; the box is on the far right, just out of shot. From the left to right the tracks read:

1. The tracks up to where the DMU is are Tuebrook Sidings and they have a connection to the Bootle branch and Seaforth Docks.

Fig. 287 is the view from the other side of the Picton Road overbridge, and Edge Hill station, which we were told on the signal box sign was 400 yards, is just visible between the two centre main lines to Runcorn and Euston. The track tamper on the left is the only vehicle in the continuation of the yard past the box. The yard on the right is a depot for the Liverpool–Manchester electrification, which includes the line we saw from Huyton through St Helens to Wigan. The Liverpool Anglican Cathedral is on the skyline.

Edge Hill signal box is 191 miles and 75 chains (308.9km) from London Euston.

Fig. 286   Edge Hill looking towards Liverpool Lime Street station, February 2015.

Fig. 287   Edge Hill looking towards the junctions and Edge Hill station, February 2015.

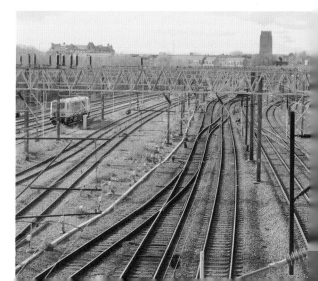

Liverpool Lime Street (LS)

Date Built	1948
LNWR Type or Builder	LMS Type 13+ Westinghouse
No. of Levers	95
Ways of Working	TCB
Current Status	Active
Listed (Y/N)	N

With all the overhead wires about in Fig. 288, an overview might be in order. Liverpool Lime Street station was constructed in a tunnel and steep cutting, one of the first such constructions in the world.

The box replaced a 135-lever LNWR box that was on the opposite side of the cutting. The box is of ARP wartime construction with 14in (35cm) solid brick walls and 12in-thick (30cm) solid concrete roof. The Westinghouse frame of ninety-five levers is of the all-electric type for power for points and signals. Interlocking is by electrical relays in a system patented in 1930. It found favour in larger railway junctions and a similar type of installation can be seen working at Crewe North Heritage Centre. Note the massively carved stone legend under the windowsill saying 'LIME STREET'. Those who have persevered through Volume 1 in this series will recall Wigan Wallgate adorned in a similar style.

The installation at Lime Street consists of thirty-one levers for points, fifty-eight for signals and six spare. Points would no doubt mean just one lever for a crossover and such like.

Fig. 289 is the view looking into the seeming void towards Edge Hill. Note how all the signals have theatre-style route indicators and some have stencil box-type captions as well. There are eventually five tracks heading up the tunnel but the middle one is a headshunt. Because of the restricted space, not all platforms are of equal length – basically the middle platforms handle the longer trains and the two

Fig. 288   Liverpool Lime Street station signal box, February 2015.

Fig. 289   Liverpool Lime Street station throat and signal box, February 2015.

Fig. 290   Liverpool Lime Street station main span, February 2015.

Fig. 291 Allerton Junction signal box, April 2013.

groups at each side the two- to three-car sets. Even so, trains at the shorter platforms can be stacked two to a platform. Liverpool Roman Catholic Cathedral is in the background; in the city it is irreverently, if humorously, referred to as 'Paddy's Wigwam'.

Fig. 290 shows the larger of the two arches at Lime Street, housing one set of local DMUs and some of the main line platforms. First TransPennine class 185 Desiro, 185 143 has arrived at platform 5, time 14:06. Looking at First TransPennine's time-table, this would be appear to be an arrival from Newcastle, two minutes early.

Liverpool Lime Street station is 193 miles 52 chains (311.6km) from London Euston.

Fig. 292 Allerton Junction and Merseyrail EMU, February 2015.

Allerton Junction (AN)

Date Built	1960
LNWR Type or Builder	BR London Midland Region Type 15
No. of Levers	70
Ways of Working	TCB
Current Status	Active
Listed (Y/N)	N

Allerton Junction is on the quadruple-track main line from Lime Street station to Runcorn and Euston. There is a double-track junction to Garston docks freightliner terminal, and the CLC line from Hunt's Cross also has a chord here although the Hunt's Cross line itself passes beneath the quadruple-track main line. Allerton was a fairly ordinary four-platform suburban station but is now Liverpool South Parkway and is the hub for Liverpool John Lennon Airport. The station is very striking, very modern and very popular. Allerton was the site of one of the first 25kV electric loco depots after Crewe, and the depot is still open. In the 1960s its allocation consisted of E3000 blue electrics.

In Fig. 291 Allerton Junction sits in the V of the four-track main line in front of the box, and the Hunt's Cross Merseyrail chord in the background. Beyond the chord is Allerton Traction and Rolling Stock Maintenance Depot.

Fig. 292 shows a Merseyrail class 507, 507 006, on the third rail electrification heading for Hunt's Cross. The opposite direction is for Lime Street, Birkenhead and Southport.

Fig. 293   Speke Junction signal box, April 2013.

Note the cast iron gradient marker post just to the right of the EMU. The quadruple tracks of the Liverpool–Euston main line head off towards Runcorn and the box is to the left.

Speke Junction (SE)

Date Built	1907
LNWR Type or Builder	LNWR Type 5+
No. of Levers	86
Ways of Working	TCB
Current Status	Active
Listed (Y/N)	N

The airport at Speke was a delightful art deco 1930s construction, and the buildings have been retained as a hotel. The airport served as RAF Speke in World War II and 'shadow' aircraft factories here constructed many planes for the RAF.

Speke Junction is in a triangle of lines formed by the Allerton Junction chord to Garston Docks, the Liverpool–Euston main line and a freight line that left the main line for the docks. Also within the triangle were extensive sidings for the docks plus a steam locomotive depot coded 8C. It was one of the last survivors, closing in May 1968. The depot handled mostly freight locos for the docks but in later years also handled a small number of passenger locos for the Liverpool Central to Manchester Central CLC Line after the CLC shed of Brunswick had closed.

There have been several boxes on the site at Speke and they were all replaced by larger structures as the railway grew until the present one, shown in Fig. 293. The wooden upper storey has been replaced by uPVC but the box is still recognizably LNWR. The lever frame is also LNWR, albeit with cut-down levers that only work switches.

South Cheshire

The schematic simplified diagram in Fig. 294 brings us back to Crewe, where we started this book; and while the boxes of Gresty No. 1 and Crewe Steelworks have been covered before, there remain four more boxes in Crewe itself and two more towards the south of the county. South Cheshire was renowned for its dairy farms but as with all else in agriculture, the situation is fluid. Our journey starts to the north, however, with Macclesfield and Winsford and then heads south, ending up at Basford Hall Junction.

Macclesfield (MD)

Date Built	1965
LNWR Type or Builder	BR London Midland Region Type 15
No. of Levers	55
Ways of Working	TCB
Current Status	Active
Listed (Y/N)	N

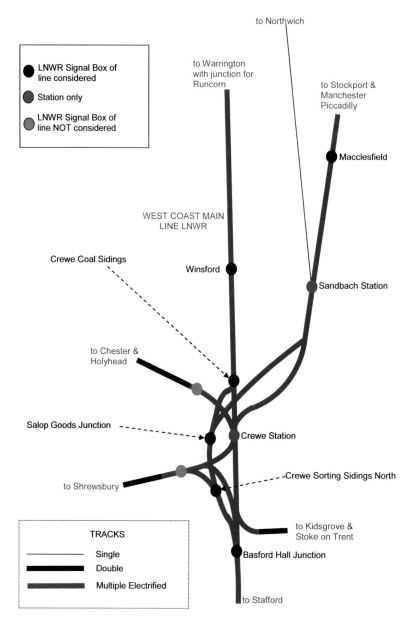

Fig. 294 South Cheshire schematic diagram.

Macclesfield grew to prominence with silk weaving, and the town's footballers are known as the 'Silkmen'. There were seventy-one silk mills in the town, and the surviving Paradise Mill can demonstrate silk 'throwing' and Jacquard weaving. Jacquard uses a system of pre-programmed punched cards that control the intricate weaving patterns needed for some finished silk cloths. The process is thought to pre-date the programmed electronic computer by around 200 years. Early electronic computers used punched cards.

Macclesfield is another of these relatively prosperous commuter towns that owes a good deal to the electric railway, and the station sees over 1¼ million passengers a year.

Fig. 295   Macclesfield signal box, December 2006.

Fig. 296   Winsford signal box, December 2014.

Fig. 295 shows that Macclesfield signal box is relatively old hat compared to the modernist station it now has. The original station was an LNWR and North Staffordshire Railway joint concern.

The only incident of any note involving the box was in 1971, when an electric multiple unit departed from the platform through a red light and ran off the track, courtesy of the trap points.

The point at which the LNWR met the North Staffordshire is the point mileages are still calculated from in Hibel Road, where there had been an early station.

Macclesfield signal box is 20 chains (400m) from the Hibel Road marker in Macclesfield.

Winsford (WD)

Date Built	1897
LNWR Type or Builder	LNWR Type 4+
No. of Levers	41
Ways of Working	TCB
Current Status	Active
Listed (Y/N)	N

When there are copious amounts of snow in Britain the TV crews come to Winsford to enquire if there is enough salt to go on the roads. This area of Cheshire has been known since Roman times for its naturally occurring salt deposits, as we have already noted at Nantwich. Winsford has a connection with Frodsham and Nantwich in that the River Weaver runs through all three. It was between Winsford and Frodsham that the river was canalized in the eighteenth century to enable the salty products to reach the sea at the River Mersey and beyond.

Fig. 296 shows Winsford signal box controlling a passing loop on the down side that is accessible to both tracks. From Crewe to just south of Winsford station the line is quadruple track. Going north, however, the line to Runcorn and Liverpool diverges within 8 miles (13km) of the box.

A northbound Virgin Pendolino speeds past. Note that there is a commodious coal bunker next to the wooden steps.

A tragic accident happened at Winsford in 1948 when a passenger on a train pulled the communication cord to stop the train, which was then hit by a following postal express. Twenty-four passengers were killed. The signaller had given Line Clear to the previous box when the train was still in section. The passenger train had pulled up short of a track circuit so couldn't be detected that way by a light in the box. Had the entire line been track circuited and the Welwyn Control in use, it would have been impossible to pull off or give Line Clear for the postal express. *See* the section on Prestatyn signal box earlier in this chapter for more information on the Welwyn Control.

Winsford signal box is 166 miles 66 chains (268.5km) from Euston.

Fig. 297   Crewe Coal Yard signal box, April 2013.

Crewe Coal Yard (CY)

Date Built	1939
LNWR Type or Builder	LMS Type 13+
No. of Levers	65
Ways of Working	TCB, AB
Current Status	Active
Listed (Y/N)	N

This is the next box south along the line from Winsford and is about ¾ mile (1.2km) outside Crewe station. With the multiplicity of lines in this area, trains are passed from Crewe signalling centre to Coal Yard using a train describer, which is a means of passing on the headcode of the train. This code is a shorthand description of where the train is going and what it consists of. The Trust computer system is a visual display of a list of trains that are expected and what their running to time situation is. The list is continually updated in real time.

The box is situated at the point where two loops from the main line, described as 'Liverpool independent', are sent round the back of Crewe station. They are then combined with two tracks from the Macclesfield/Manchester direction – 'Manchester independent' – to form the connection for Shrewsbury via Salop Goods Junction, to which the box works AB, and then to the main groups of freight sidings and loops near where Crewe Sorting Sidings North signal box is.

Crewe Coal Sidings signal box is 158 miles 68 chains (255.6km) from London Euston.

Salop Goods Junction (SG)

Date Built	1901
LNWR Type or Builder	LNWR Type 4
No. of Levers	65
Ways of Working	TCB, AB
Current Status	Active
Listed (Y/N)	N

The layout and facilities at Crewe were remodelled from 1896 to 1907, and this box dates from those works. The layout is much the same now although some of it has been cut back.

The lines described as Liverpool and Manchester independent are usually freight only to avoid congestion at Crewe station. However, when summer excursion trains were run that didn't need to stop at Crewe they would often be routed on the freight-only lines and passengers got to see the extensive marshalling yards – a move bound to delight some and puzzle others.

Salop Goods Junction, as its name implies, passed freights to Gresty Lane No. 1 box and out onto the Shrewsbury line, Salopia being the Latin name for Shropshire. Passenger trains from Shrewsbury make their way to Crewe station

Fig. 298   Salop Goods Junction signal box, December 2014.

Fig. 299   Crewe Sorting Sidings North signal box, February 2015.

directly from Gresty Lane No. 1 and Crewe power box to the station.

Passing the box in Fig. 298 are six lines, two from Liverpool, two from Manchester and two originally from Chester but now a spur onto the Chester line and a siding.

Salop Goods Junction signal box is 157 miles 71 chains (254.1km) from London Euston.

Crewe Sorting Sidings North (SSN)

Date Built	1962
LNWR Type or Builder	BR London Midland Region Type 15
No. of Levers	IFS panel
Ways of Working	AB, TCB
Current Status	Active
Listed (Y/N)	N

Part of the Modernization Plan of 1955 was to construct massive new marshalling yards to handle the huge numbers of wagon- and part wagon-load freight trains that moved most of the nation's stuff around the country. Although these yards were not entirely new in the 1960s they rapidly lost their usefulness as traffic switched to roads. Part of the reason for this was that the network had been cut back so it was no longer possible to dispatch goods locally – goods had to be taken part of the journey by road to get them to a dispatch point and at the other end the goods would also need to finish their journey by road. This made wagon-load freight trains uneconomic, and, because of the multiple handling stops, usually slower. There were half-hearted attempts to put containers on rail and then on a lorry chassis, and British Road Services were supposed to fill the gaps left by railway closure, but it was to no avail.

However some yards still survive and have found other uses now that wagon load freight trains have been consigned to history and the preserved railways.

Much of the yard and a box that controlled it has survived at Crewe (Fig. 299). This box has an unusual way of working absolute block. There are nine reception sidings allocated to receiving trains. The signaller can select Line Clear for, say, no. 1 siding. When that siding has been occupied, the signaller can select Line Clear for siding 2 even though there is already a train technically in the section at siding 1, and so on. This kind of working is known as 'permissive' and was common throughout the network where there were yards and multiple sidings. Track circuit lights, which normally light up to show where a train is on the diagram, are replicated above the block instruments to assist the Line Clear selections.

The working out of the yard is also absolute block to Basford Hall Junction signal box.

Part of the yard is shown in Fig. 300. From left to right:

- On the far left is a container train that has arrived from the south on the down independent.
- After that is a fan of thirty loops, not under the wires, and class 66s are in evidence.
- The box in the foreground is the derelict Middle Sidings box; it divides the up arrival roads which, by the time they've got to the box, are the up departure roads. Immediately above the Middle Sidings box roof is a white rectangular shape and this is the North Sorting box top at the other end of the yard.
- To the right of the middle box are a couple of parked class 70s and behind them is the ballast stockpile and another container train.

Fig. 300 Crewe Sorting Sidings North overview, February 2015.

- To the fore is another class 70 hiding behind some ballast hoppers.
- To the right of that is where the sleeper pile begins.
- Finally, on the far right, is the West Coast Main Line, just out of Crewe station.

Crewe Sorting Sidings North signal box is 157 miles 23 chains (253.1km) from London Euston.

Basford Hall Junction (BH)

Date Built	1897
LNWR Type or Builder	LNWR Type 4
No. of Levers	48
Ways of Working	TCB, AB
Current Status	Active
Listed (Y/N)	N

The independent goods lines that entered Crewe Sorting Sidings emerge at Basford Hall Junction, which works absolute block to Crewe Sorting Sidings North signal box and TCB to Crewe power box and Stoke-on-Trent power box.

In Fig. 301 the nearest two tracks are down independent, fast and slow, and up from that is the up line, which is about to split into fast and slow. After that come the quadruple-track main lines.

Basford Hall Junction signal box is 156 miles 23 chains (251.5km) from Euston station.

Staffordshire

Staffordshire is synonymous with pottery and ceramics, but also had heavy engineering in Wolverhampton and Stafford, as well as cars at Tamworth.

The simplified schematic diagram in Fig. 302 shows a fragmented disposition of signal boxes with little mechanical signalling or absolute block working. Staffordshire was home to the North Staffordshire Railway, covered in Volume 1, and the Great Western at Wolverhampton, covered in the GWR book. The LNWR ran through the middle of it, and the Midland Railway got in on the act too.

Fig. 301 Basford Hall Junction signal box, February 2015.

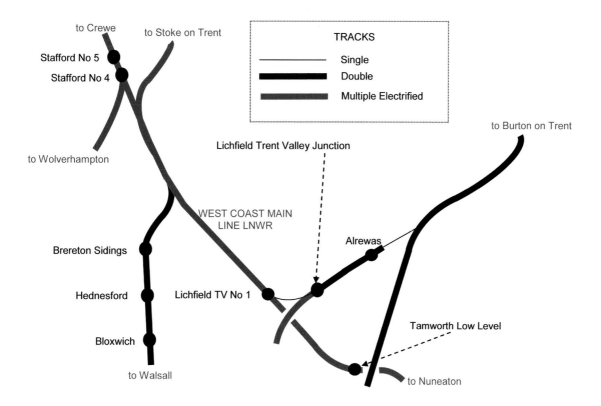

Fig. 302   Staffordshire area schematic diagram.

Altogether it was fascinating pot pourri of railways, of which some traces remain. The general path of the fragmented journeys will be north to south; some of West Midlands county is also included in this section.

Stafford No. 5 (SD5)

Date Built	1952
LNWR Type or Builder	BR London Midland Region Type 14
No. of Levers	150
Ways of Working	TCB
Current Status	Active
Listed (Y/N)	N

Stafford is an important administrative centre for the county and an attractive town, with many fine buildings and long history.

Fig. 303   Stafford No. 5 signal box, March 2007.

Originally famous for footwear, Stafford was later well known for heavy industry, from large-scale power transformers to locomotives, with the English Electric company. American-owned Perkins has a diesel engine factory here. The 'Evode' works produced a pungent smell in the town as well as jobs making Evo-Stik adhesive, and that continues with Bostik.

There remains a large MOD depot that was once RAF Stafford, which was the Youth Selection Centre and a storage facility for aircraft equipment.

Stafford station was once a busy junction, with lines running in from Shrewsbury and Uttoxeter. The Salop branch still exists as a siding, and there is still a junction with the line to Wolverhampton.

Stafford No. 5 (Fig. 303) is one of the largest boxes on the network at 150 levers, and is a class 7 box classification for signaller working. Boxes are classified according to their size and how busy they are – the higher the classification, the more money the signaller is paid. The box has two London Midland Region maroon signs, one a box name plate and the other a reminder that Stafford station is only 150yd away. These reminders were put at signal box locations where trains might be held at signals to reassure passengers that the station was not far away; we saw another survivor at Edge Hill. Note also the GEC works in the background, who succeeded English Electric, builders of many diesel electric locomotives. The view is towards Crewe.

Stafford No. 5 signal box is 133 miles 57 chains (215.2km) from London Euston.

Stafford No. 4 (SD4)

Date Built	1960
LNWR Type or Builder	BR London Midland Type 15
No. of Levers	105
Ways of Working	TCB
Current Status	Active
Listed (Y/N)	N

Stafford No. 4 signal box, despite having the lower lever count, is at what could be called the business end of Stafford station. There were two goods yards, one on the up and the other on the down side, where, not surprisingly, up is towards Euston. After the down yard the double-track branch to Wolverhampton trails the down main line, and there are a total of eight crossovers for trains to access the branch and change platforms at the station. There are six platforms, of which five are

Fig. 304   Stafford No. 4 signal box, April 2013.

in use, and there were more in the days of the two branches referred to above. There was also a Royal Mail depot, as Stafford's central hub location made it a magnet for mail. The station dates from 1962.

The box, shown in Fig. 304, is a Type 15 on steroids – this must be the largest example of the species, and it is extremely busy, with hundreds of train movements per day and two signallers on duty to handle them. It is interesting to note that a good deal of point work on the WCML is electrically operated but here there is still quite a lot of point rodding at the survey date. The vehicle on the arrival road of what had been the down yard looks like a ballast tamper machine. The view is towards Euston and is from the Newport Road overbridge; presumably the Newport referred to is the one in Shropshire.

Stafford No. 4 signal box is 133 miles 32 chains (214.7km) from London Euston.

The Chase Line

The line is situated at the beginning of Cannock Chase, an area of heathland that was hunted for deer in medieval times and was the scene of much coal mining activity in later years. The Chase has been designated an Area of Outstanding Natural Beauty. The line has been converted to operate TCB and none of the signal boxes depicted is in position any longer.

Brereton Sidings (BS)

Date Built	1908
LNWR Type or Builder	LNWR Type 5
No. of Levers	20
Ways of Working	AB
Current Status	Closed and moved November 2013
Listed (Y/N)	N

Brereton Sidings signal box was off the end of Rugeley Town station. The box, as well as being a block post, also supervised working to Rugeley B power station.

The box depicted in Fig. 305 is in fine fettle; the Chasewater Railway clearly also thought so, as they paid for its removal to their site after it was donated to them by Network Rail. Network Rail also gave some of the signalling equipment from the line. The box is apparently currently stored at their Brownhills West station.

Those who have read the GWR book in this series may recall that coal trains from Avonmouth Dock made their way up the Hereford–Shrewsbury line to Rugeley power station, and this is the end of that journey. Both Craven Arms and Shrewsbury saw such trains.

Fig. 306 is the view from Rugeley Town station footbridge towards the power station sidings, back to the junction with the WCML. The distant signal is fixed and used to be from Colwich signal box's panel. Below that, on the same post, is a ground disc that signalled entry into the power station, the points and crossover for which are just around the curve. Behind the main signal post is another containing two power station siding signals. The smaller-armed signal in the distance is the power station siding exit signal. Note the two buffer stops in the undergrowth. There had been a colliery here at Brereton and a further colliery at Lea Hall, off the power station branch.

Brereton Sidings signal box was 13 miles 27 chains (21.5km) from Ryecroft Junction, near Walsall.

Fig. 305   Brereton Sidings signal box, March 2007.

Fig. 306   Brereton Sidings signals for the power station and former colliery, March 2007.

Hednesford (HD)

Date Built	1877
LNWR Type or Builder	LNWR Type 4
No. of Levers	38
Ways of Working	AB
Current Status	Closed and moved February 2014
Listed (Y/N)	N

Hednesford was home to the West Cannock Colliery company, who had at least five mines in the area, and there had been at least three signal boxes in Hednesford to control the output from the workings.

The signal box at Hednesford, and originally No. 1, was a venerable and – by the look of it in Fig. 307

Fig. 307   Hednesford signal box, March 2007.

Fig. 308   Hednesford signal box signals, March 2007.

Fig. 309   Bloxwich signal box and cautionary ground signal, March 2007.

– much cherished structure, as it was donated to Hednesford for their park by Network Rail. The box is shown with planters and a garden so perhaps a park environment is appropriate.

They hope to fully restore the box, complete with a partial frame operating a few signals, and use it as an educational resource.

In Fig. 308 all that is left of extensive colliery sidings are the usual birch trees. The line is shown heading off to Rugeley.

Hednesford signal box was 9 miles 12 chains (14.7km) from Ryecroft Junction near Walsall.

Bloxwich (BH)

Date Built	1959
LNWR Type or Builder	BR London Midland Region Type 15
No. of Levers	30
Ways of Working	AB
Current Status	Demolished 2013
Listed (Y/N)	N

Bloxwich is actually in the county of West Midlands and is a district of Walsall. Like Walsall, it built up a reputation for coal mining and iron smelting. Forge shops sprang up to manufacture all sorts of worked ironware, mostly smaller hardware items, while Walsall established a reputation for lock- and key-making.

Bloxwich has been blessed with two railway stations: the box was close to Bloxwich, while Bloxwich North is within a mile.

The box was the now familiar LMR Type 15, and perhaps it was too familiar, as it is the only one of the three on the Chase Line to have been demolished.

Fig. 309 shows an unusual yellow-striped ground disc in front of the box. This is a kind of 'permissive' signal, in that trains could pass it at caution, as opposed to a red-striped disc, which must not be passed at danger. The reason for this was to allow shunting movements to take place along that piece of track that did not require the signal to be selected off all the time before a train could pass it. There may be many such movements and the yellow disc saves delay and wear and tear on the signals. They are usually only fitted where the signaller has the signal in clear view. There was a loop line in front of the box, leading to private sidings.

Fig. 310   The vista towards Bloxwich station, March 2007.

Fig. 310 is the view towards Bloxwich station, with the private siding, known as Thomas's, on the left. The ground disc for a reversing move over the trailing crossover is on the left and the home signal to protect the crossing to the right.

Bloxwich signal box was 2 miles 6 chains (3.3km) from Ryecroft Junction near Walsall.

Back on the West Coast Main Line now, we come to Lichfield Trent Valley No. 1.

Lichfield Trent Valley No. 1

Date Built	1911
LNWR Type or Builder	LNWR Type 5+
No. of Levers	80
Ways of Working	TCB
Current Status	Demolished June 2007
Listed (Y/N)	N

The city of Lichfield is famous for its medieval cathedral with three spires. There are over 230 listed buildings in Lichfield and a host of Georgian buildings of note and character. Samuel Johnson was possibly its most famous resident, and described Lichfield as the 'city of philosophers'. It has seen limited commercial development and retains its charm and attractiveness.

Lichfield TV No. 1 signal box has only about eight months to go in Fig. 311 but looks quite cheerful. It has an LMR maroon name board, locking frame windows and, although given the full uPVC treatment, looks every inch an LNWR box.

The box was in between the tracks at Lichfield TV station. One of the fast lines has a 110mph marker board.

The box was involved in an unusual accident in January 1946. The signaller was known to use all his weight to move the levers over in the box, and due to a mismatch of LNWR and LMS components it was just possible to defeat the locking and pull off home signals when every other condition was against it. This resulted in a rear end collision when an express fish train from Fleetwood ran into the back of a Stafford–Nuneaton stopping passenger train. There were twenty deaths and twenty-one injuries.

The situation had been exacerbated by the failure of a locking bar to move due to frozen ground trapping the point rodding and preventing movement. Another contributory factor was thought to be the amount that the down rod from the lever was able to flex due to the extreme height of the frame. Aided and abetted by the weather, this freak accident was never repeated.

Lichfield TV No 1 signal box was 116 miles 22 chains (187.1km) from London Euston.

Fig. 311   Lichfield Trent Valley No. 1 signal box, October 2007.

Lichfield Trent Valley Junction (TV)

Date Built	1897
LNWR Type or Builder	LNWR Type 4
No. of Levers	45
Ways of Working	TCB
Current Status	Active
Listed (Y/N)	N

The station junction at Lichfield is divided into Low Level for the WCML, Trent Valley; and a single High Level platform for the South Staffs line, which runs between Birmingham New Street and Burton-on-Trent. There is a single-track chord and TV Junction is at the end of that, with a crossover to acquire the single platform. The High Level platform is the passenger terminus of the 'City' line to Birmingham and this is as far as the 25kV electrification reaches.

Fig. 312   Lichfield Trent Valley Junction signal box, October 2007.

Fig. 313   Alrewas signal box, October 2007.

There is a further station called Lichfield City about 1½ miles (2.5km) towards Birmingham.

The box in Fig. 312 looks well kept, again with locking frame windows a feature. There are modernized windows, steps and toilet block but only one finial. This box and its partner at Alrewas were supposed to go in 2016, but it seems there may be a reprieve until 2017. Most of the levers within are painted white. This box was, apparently, the last to have a coal stove, which was only removed a few years ago.

Alrewas (AS)

Date Built	1899
LNWR Type or Builder	LNWR Type 4
No. of Levers	IFS panel
Ways of Working	TCB
Current Status	Active
Listed (Y/N)	N

Alrewas is a large village that finds itself at the junction of the Trent and Mersey Canal and the River Trent, both massive trade arteries in their day. The National Memorial Arboretum is close by.

The box in Fig. 313 controlled the manually operated barriers next to it, and also the operation of the point and associated signals for the line going to single track to cross the River Trent and then joining up with the double-track line from Derby to Birmingham. The box suffered a fire in 2005 but the signalling was undamaged. The signaller was accommodated in a temporary building and had to rush out to attend to trains while the repairs were being carried out on the box structure.

Tamworth Low Level (TH)

Date Built	1910
LNWR Type or Builder	LNWR Type 4
No. of Levers	35
Ways of Working	TCB
Current Status	Demolished
Listed (Y/N)	N

Tamworth's main claim to fame was the Reliant car factory, which made the three-wheeled Robin and the contrasting Scimitar sports car for decades – the latter was a favourite of HRH Princess Royal. The factory closed in 2001 but Tamworth survives on a diet of clothing and paper manufacture together with engineering, and brick and tile works.

Tamworth Low Level signal box (Fig. 314) was a casualty of the quadrupling of the lines between Stafford and Rugby. There had been a road crossing at Hademore together with signal box but that was replaced by a road overbridge and the box demolished.

In 1870 there was an accident at Tamworth where the Irish Mail was diverted into a siding due to a signaller's error, compounded by the then lack of proper interlocking. Signals were alleged to be off for the express but the points were not interlocked with them and the road was incorrectly set. There were also criticisms over the block instruments and lack of an accurate timepiece in the box.

Death and injury resulted from this event, with three dead and twelve injured.

Tamworth signal box was 110 miles 12 chains (177.3km) from London Euston.

The rest of the signal boxes that existed in LNWR territory do not fit into a defined geographical area and their survival has been down to a quirk of fate or circumstance. These last boxes will be covered north to south.

Fig. 314   Tamworth Low Level signal box, October 2007.

and waste, and there were thirty-one shoddy mills in the town. Michael Portillo visited the town on one of his Great Railway Journeys. The station and signal box are on the Huddersfield–Leeds line. The LNWR had a presence in Leeds, with engine sheds at Farnley Junction. The terminus platforms at Leeds City station were where the LNWR line trains terminated, the station being a joint one with the Midland and North Eastern Railways.

The box in Fig. 315 is a gate box and was formerly named 'Lady Anne's Crossing' but was made a block post in 1952. The gates are manually worked over a narrow road with difficult sighting for traffic, and this has presumably helped the box survive as an LNWR outpost – although it is slated for closure in 2017.

West Yorkshire

Batley (B)

Date Built	1887
LNWR Type or Builder	LNWR Type 4
No. of Levers	IFS panel
Ways of Working	TCB
Current Status	Active
Listed (Y/N)	N

Batley had a considerable presence in the 'shoddy trade', which was reclamation of wool from rags

Fig. 315   Batley signal box, July 2012.

Fig. 316   Watery Lane Shunt Frame signal box, November 2008.

South Midlands

Watery Lane Shunt Frame (WL)

Date Built	1942
LNWR Type or Builder	LMS Type 13
No. of Levers	IFS panel
Ways of Working	Shunting
Current Status	Demolished 2012
Listed (Y/N)	N

This box controlled a couple of goods loops on the Birmingham New Street–Wolverhampton High Level LNWR line (Fig. 316). The box had been out of use for some years before it was demolished. It was situated between Tipton and Dudley Port stations in the West Midlands, where the inland Dudley was a canal hub. Part of this infrastructure forms the Black Country Museum together with the remains of forty coal pits, railway and much other industrial heritage to make up an accurate picture of one of the first industrial landscapes in Britain.

Narborough (NH)

Date Built	1887
LNWR Type or Builder	LNWR Type 3+
No. of Levers	IFS panel
Ways of Working	AB
Current Status	Closed 2006
Listed (Y/N)	N

Moving eastwards, there were a couple of boxes on the Leicester–Nuneaton line. Narborough is a village that is near the junction of several road systems and enjoys a station complete with waiting room and original buildings. The station had closed in the 1960s but local objections led to it being reopened although the local authority had to pay to have the station recommissioned. There's no mechanical signalling here and the box had already closed at the time of the visit, but in Fig. 317 it looks better than many that are still open – the local parish council have had a lot to do with that.

The cock's comb ridge tiles are an unusual survivor, and the box is also unusual in having no locking frame windows. The brick base looks as though it has been rebuilt at some point.

The Travis Perkins yard over the road houses the original goods shed.

Croft (CT)

Date Built	1901
LNWR Type or Builder	LNWR Type 4
No. of Levers	Westcad VDU
Ways of Working	TCB
Current Status	Active
Listed (Y/N)	N

Fig. 317   Narborough signal box, March 2008.

This box was originally called Croft Sidings, and the sidings in question are concerned with a quarry that produces stone for onward transport by rail. Stalwart readers of the Midland Railway part of Volume 1 of this book may recall that Bardon Hill box in Leicestershire was serving the same function.

When the line was resignalled in 2006, the mechanical frame was removed and the whole line controlled by a computerized display using a computer screen display to represent the track and signals, and a trackerball, which is basically a non-moving mouse, to make switch selections.

We now head further south to the Coventry–Nuneaton line.

Coundon Road Station

Date Built	1876
LNWR Type or Builder	LNWR Type 4+
No. of Levers	22
Ways of Working	AB
Current Status	Demolished January 2014
Listed (Y/N)	N

Coundon Road station in Coventry had closed in 1965 but the name was to live on with the signal box for almost another fifty years; traces of the platforms survived at the survey date in 2007. The box was closed on 23 May 2009, when the line was resignalled, but it survived almost another five

Fig. 318   Croft signal box, March 2008.

years after the last train had been signalled. In Fig. 319 the planters have a spring look to them. Once again, as at Narborough, there are no locking frame windows. The London Taxis/Carbodies plant is behind the box.

Fig. 320 looks like an engineer's possession of the line, which means that no service trains can pass. The platform of the former Coundon Road station is visible. There was a nearby Daimler Halt built

Fig. 320   Former Coundon Road station platform and signals, March 2007.

Fig. 319   Coundon Road Station signal box, March 2007.

by the LNWR in 1917 solely for employees of the Daimler car company; it closed in 1965. Daimler manufactured armoured cars as well as limousines. There was no public access to the halt.

Coundon Road Station signal box was 1 mile 3 chains (1.7km) from Coventry North Junction.

Hawkesbury Lane

Date Built	1896
LNWR Type or Builder	LNWR Type 4+
No. of Levers	26
Ways of Working	AB
Current Status	Demolished
Listed (Y/N)	N

Fig. 321   Hawkesbury Lane signal box, March 2007.

Hawkesbury Lane is near Bedworth station in Warwickshire. The town of Bedworth was another bastion of coal mining, with the last colliery not closing until 1994. The box was actually on Blackhorse Road in Bedworth.

The box has fared quite well in Fig. 321, with only the galvanized steps and uPVC windows giving the modern game away.

The box supervised a manually controlled barrier crossing as at Coundon Road but also had a couple of sets of private sidings, with their associated crossovers, to control.

Fig. 322 shows the view towards Nuneaton. The box is on the opposite side of the line and road to the rather gentrified crossing keeper's cottage, just in view on the right. The view is also towards the Calor Gas sidings, which are not themselves in view although the crossover for them is. Note the signal post on the sidings side of the line without any arms, now in use as a guy wire tethering post. The bracket signal subsidiary arm allows a train into the Hawkesbury Lane up sidings beyond the road and crossing.

Fig. 322   Hawkesbury Lane signal box crossover and signals, March 2007.

CHAPTER 3

Caledonian Railway (CR)

The Caledonian Railway was a major Scottish railway company that linked Glasgow and England, and still does through the West Coast Main Line and the LNWR. Volume 1 of the LMSR books covered the Midland Railway route to Carlisle and the Glasgow and South Western route to Glasgow. The third route was by the North Eastern Railway and North British to Edinburgh, and that will be covered in the LNER books in this series together with the Great North of Scotland Railway, which took the LNER into the Highlands.

The CR developed a multiplicity of lines and intensive suburban services around Glasgow and took passengers onto their own ferries for the Western Isles and Argyllshire.

The CR also forayed north to Stirling, Perth and Aberdeen and had a presence in Edinburgh, so pretty much covered the country except the far north, which was the preserve of the Highland Railway and the GNoSR.

The railway had substantial interests in the Lanarkshire coalfield and went into Dumfriesshire after the iron ore there. It had an alliance with the Maryport and Carlisle Railway, which became subsumed into the LNWR in Cumbria.

When the railways were grouped in 1923, the Caledonian Railway was capitalized at £57 million and had 2,827 route miles (4,550km) of track. A double-track main line was counted as double the mileage.

In common with most modern major cities and centres, Glasgow and Edinburgh have hardly any and no CR signalling presence respectively. The lesser main lines north and east are much more fruitful.

Clyde–Forth Valley to Perth

This corridor of activity and population is an intrinsic part of the economy – the canal system, and later railways, developed the coal, iron and steel industries. Falkirk was a notable centre and a prosperous one, with many fine nineteenth-century buildings. Falkirk still has a hand in heavier industries with Alexander Dennis, who manufacture buses and fire engines. More recently, the area moved into a different kind of energy with the Grangemouth refinery and associated petrochemical works.

Falkirk has also found fame with the Falkirk Wheel, which is a spectacular inter-canal boat transport mechanism. The only equivalent in England is the Anderton Boat Lift in Cheshire.

The Caledonian Railway is intermingled with its rival the North British in the valley, but breaks clear to head north to Stirling and Perth on its own. The North British had its own route to Perth. The area at

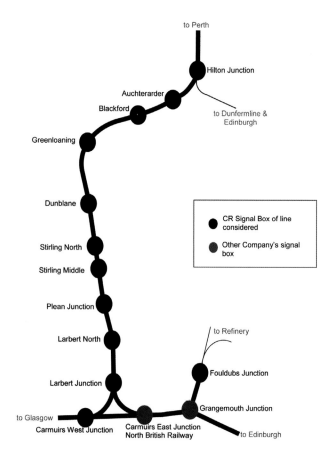

Fig. 323 Caledonian Railway, Forth Valley–Perth schematic diagram.

Legend:
- ● CR Signal Box of line considered
- ● Other Company's signal box

Schematic labels:
- to Perth
- Hilton Junction
- Auchterarder
- Blackford
- to Dunfermline & Edinburgh
- Greenloaning
- Dunblane
- Stirling North
- Stirling Middle
- Plean Junction
- Larbert North
- to Refinery
- Larbert Junction
- Fouldubs Junction
- Grangemouth Junction
- to Glasgow
- Carmuirs West Junction
- Carmuirs East Junction North British Railway
- to Edinburgh

Fig. 324 Carmuirs West Junction signal box, September 2007.

Camelon was where the Union Canal met the Forth and Clyde Canal with a lock flight. The locks have been replaced with the Falkirk Wheel.

Carmuirs West Junction passed trains from the Glasgow area north to Perth and beyond.

The box, shown in Fig. 324, worked AB to Greenhill Junction and AB to Carmuirs East Junction and Larbert Junction. Note the tacked-on admin block, as a box this old and this small would not have been built with toilet facilities. Note also the painted or treated brickwork to keep out the ravages of winter. The Glasgow direction is to the right.

Carmuirs West Junction signal box was 108 miles 76 chains (175.3km) from Carlisle, where the Caledonian Railway southern extent starts at Citadel station.

Larbert Junction (LJ)

Date Built	c.1871
CR Type or Builder	Caledonian Non-Standard
No. of Levers	40
Ways of Working	AB
Current Status	Closed
Listed (Cat/N)	N

Larbert Junction met the same fate as Carmuirs West, in the sense that all semaphore signals were removed but the box has been retained as a school to instruct signallers in using a lever frame. It had been usual to have examples of signals as well, but this clearly presents difficulties when the box is close to the running lines.

the starting point was just beginning to be modernized at the survey date, a process that is now largely complete. Historic Scotland categorizes listed buildings and structures using the ABC classification, as described in the introduction.

Carmuirs West Junction (CW)

Date Built	1881
CR Type or Builder	Caledonian Non-Standard
No. of Levers	20
Ways of Working	AB
Current Status	Demolished
Listed (Cat/N)	N

Fig. 325   Larbert Junction signal box, September 2007.

Fig. 326   Larbert North signal box, September 2007.

Fig. 325 shows Larbert Junction signal box; the name plate was below the end window. The Falkirk Wheel is out of shot to the left and to the rear.

Larbert Junction signal box is 109 miles 41 chains (176.2km) from Carlisle and 26 miles 35 chains (42.5km) from Edinburgh Dalry Road station.

Larbert North (LN)

Date Built	1892
CR Type or Builder	Caledonian Type N2
No. of Levers	59
Ways of Working	AB
Current Status	Active
Listed (Cat/N)	N

Larbert North, however, does have some mechanical signalling. Larbert station is close by and there is some trackwork to signal. On the down side is a pair of goods loops and on the up side a goods loop and engineer's sidings. 'Down' on this line means towards Perth.

In Fig. 326 the box has the signs of locking frame windows with arches and window sills but they are bricked up. The brick-built outhouse does not have the brickwork treatment, which is where one might suppose it is needed the most. Wooden steps complete a period scene. When the box is viewed from the Muirhall Road in Larbert you can see where the coal-fired stove was by the replacement slates on the roof.

Larbert North signal box nestles against the stone wall that runs parallel with the Muirhall Road. In Fig. 327, note that there are concrete troughs on the down side for the newly installed colour light signals back at the triangular junction.

The view here is towards Stirling and Perth.

Larbert station has a memorial plaque to commemorate the Quintinshill disaster – while Larbert was not directly involved, it was the place from which the 7th Royal Scots cavalry regiment set off to fight in World War I.

In 1915 Quintinshill was a wayside station with loop lines on the CR main line south, past Gretna

Fig. 327   Larbert North signal box and signals, September 2007.

to Carlisle. A local passenger train left Carlisle and was followed by two express trains from the south.

A goods train had been held inside the down loop so the passenger train was crossed over to the up main line in order to give the expresses a clear run past. A further goods train of coal empties was diverted into the up loop. So out of four lines passing the box, two of them loops, three were occupied by stationary trains.

One of the expresses was closing in, and the signaller gave Line Clear for the down line, which was the only line that was clear.

The signaller then cleared signals for the troop train containing the 7th Royal Scots and their horses to proceed south from Larbert on the up line. The troop train collided with the local passenger train standing on the up main line. Into this scene of carnage hurtled the down express, ploughing into the wreckage that was strewn across the running lines.

Wooden, gas-lit coaches and the sheer violence with which the two collisions took place resulted in 226 fatalities and 246 injuries. Many of the 7th Royal Scots horses perished as well.

Two signallers in the box at the time were convicted of culpable homicide.

There were lever collars provided, which, when placed over a lever, remind the signaller not to pull the lever, and in some cases prevent it from being pulled over. These were not used. The later innovations of track circuiting and Welwyn Control would have prevented such a disaster and their introduction was hastened by such events.

Larbert North signal box is 110 miles 30 chains (177.6km) from Carlisle.

Plean Junction (PJ)

Date Built	*c.*1870
CR Type or Builder	Caledonian Type N1
No. of Levers	26
Ways of Working	AB
Current Status	Closed
Listed (Cat/N)	N

Fig. 328   Plean Junction signal box, September 2007.

Plean Junction was the junction for Alloa station, which was closed in 1968 but reopened in 2008, though the line now runs from Stirling.

The signal box in Fig. 328 is a tall structure that affords a view over the bridge that the camera is on. The tacked-on extension and girders to support it were probably done at the same time as the corrugated roof. Note the 1970s-style stick-on modernistic name plate. This box too has the arched locking frame windows, at least two sets, bricked up. There is a tunnel from the box for point rodding but none coming out at this stage. There had been a facing crossover to access the Scottish Timber Products factory sidings, so four points in all.

The view in Fig. 329 is from the same bridge again, towards Larbert. The bracket signal has lost its arms and the former sidings exit road can just be seen on the left, but the up running line on the left has been plain lined.

There was a collision at Plean Junction in January 1951. The up side towards Larbert had suffered a telegraph pole falling across the signal wire of the up distant signal, which had the effect of pulling the signal off, or clear. Further telegraph

Fig. 329   Plean Junction signals looking towards Larbert, September 2007.

Fig. 330   Plean Junction signal looking towards Stirling, September 2007.

poles fell, and one cut off all block instrument communications. Trains had to be passed by using a time interval system, and all drivers had to be cautioned verbally by a track ganger at the line side.

An ex-LMS Black Five 4–6–0 loco had been brought to a stand at the Alloa junction home signal to allow a passenger train from Alloa to precede it. Into this scene, doing about 35mph (55km/h), came another Black Five with a passenger train, and as the distant signal was off (from the telegraph pole across the wire), was putting on steam around the bend to the junction. The collision on rails wet with snow was inevitable at that speed, and two people were killed and fourteen others injured.

There were verbal communication breakdowns but the driver of the passenger train was hauled over the coals as he was aware that he was driving under special regulations and as such should have ignored signals at clear as they could be faulty.

In Fig. 330, on the right, by the home signal, is where the passenger train came round the curve towards the camera. In Fig. 329, just before the old junction on the left and at the very bottom of the picture, is where the light engine was standing and where the collision took place.

With the usual benefit of hindsight, it might have been better if the ganger had been dispatched up the line to cut the distant signal wire at the post to return it to danger, thus possibly averting the accident.

Plean Junction signal box is 114 miles 26 chains (184km) from Carlisle.

Stirling Middle (SM)

Date Built	1901
CR Type or Builder	Caledonian Type N2
No. of Levers	96, Nx panel
Ways of Working	AB
Current Status	Active
Listed (Cat/N)	A

Stirling is a city steeped in royal history, with a towering castle and fortifications as well as the Wallace monument. The city is the ancient capital of Scotland, and the Great Hall and Renaissance Palace are visible reminders of this. Stirling is also an administrative centre with a renowned university, and has attracted financial services companies.

Stirling is a natural junction for the road system as well as a crossing point for the River Forth. These

Fig. 331   Stirling Middle signal box, October 2014.

Fig. 332 *Stirling Middle signal box and signals, August 2003.*

Fig. 333 *Stirling Middle signals on platform ends, August 2003.*

Fig. 332 is looking back to Plean Junction. The triple-bracket lattice post signal by the box is for the three roads that depart the station for the south. These three roads have fused from a total of five platforms at the photograph date. The arrival signals from the south with their backs to us and the two signals with distant signals on the same post are through roads, and the other a bay platform. The distants will be Stirling North's distant signals, advising a driver of the status of the next home signal in the station, which will be Stirling North's. Each through road also has a calling on arm to caution a train into a platform that may be already occupied, or authorize shunting only. A ballast tamper machine is in the siding by the box.

Fig. 333 shows the south end of Stirling station and platform starters for the south. Here are three generations of railway signalling. On the far platform is a modernized Network Rail home signal with galvanized ladders and safety hoops. After that is an LMS-pattern bracket signal, and finally a Caledonian-pattern lattice post signal with additional lattice post support. The Network Rail innovation is the arrows advising drivers of which signal is relevant to which platform. All the signals look as though they are motor worked, although the box is not far up the line.

Fig. 334 gives a glimpse of the listed Stirling station and an idea of the sighting issues posed by platform canopies. The home signal at the end of platform 2, where the camera is, is on a low post. It looks as though there had been a taller signal there, as there is evidence of whitewash on the road overbridge. There is another lattice post bracket signal for the bay platforms to depart to the north, towards Perth. The Alloa line reinstatement came after this visit.

Stirling North box can be seen on the left, and opposite the box a class 66 is making its way to the platform 3 through road.

An EWS-branded class 66, 66 028, trundles past platform 3 with a short engineer's train in Fig. 335. The siding by the platform 2 home signal was another bay platform but is now just a siding with a

ancient travel routes usually bear fruit in railway terms, and Stirling station is a magnificent survivor of the golden age of railways; it too is listed by Historic Scotland. There is also an old engine shed and a train crew lodging house.

The box in Fig. 331 is an imposing one – and all the more so when you realize that there is another one like it at the other end of the station.

The larger Caledonian Railway signal boxes favour a lookout similar to a guard's ducket on an early railway coach that allows the signallers to see up the line without opening a window. The bricked-up locking frame window portals with the arches to them can be seen quite easily. Unusually, not only have the chimney stacks survived but they have terracotta pots to them. The wooden steps complete a period feel that is worthy of the box's listing.

ground disc exit. The two inner bay platforms look a bit agricultural at this date.

Stirling Middle also now controls the reactivated and updated Stirling–Alloa–Kincardine route (SAK) by use of a TEW mosaic mimic panel with integrated CCTV monitors for crossing controls. The mimic panel is a diagrammatic form of control panel that integrates signalling control into the diagram; as it is made up of a tiled mosaic pattern, the panel is relatively easily changed. TEW of Nottingham also supply passenger train describer boards as well as signal box equipment.

Stirling Middle is 118 miles 18 chains (190.3km) from Carlisle.

Stirling North (SN)

Date Built	1900
CR Type or Builder	Caledonian Type N2
No. of Levers	48+
Ways of Working	AB
Current Status	Active
Listed (Cat/N)	A

Eleven years on from the previous view, Fig. 336 shows Stirling North. This is in the same class as Middle but the lever count is halved at forty-eight; this has been reduced over the years and the partial closure of the Alloa and Kincardine branch no doubt had an influence. The branch reopened in 2008 and

Fig. 334   Stirling station, North signal box and signals, August 2003.

Fig. 335   Stirling station with a class 66 on a short train, August 2003.

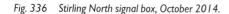

Fig. 336   Stirling North signal box, October 2014.

Fig. 337   Stirling North signal box and environs, October 2014.

this view post-dates the reopening. The ground disc was mentioned in Fig. 335 and is used to exit the siding that runs a short way parallel with platform 2. Note the double-railed trap points designed to derail a SPAD or runaway vehicle. Nearly all the mechanical signalling we have seen has now been removed.

Fig. 337 pans back to the double-track main line towards Perth. The down main is off for a train. Over on the right, the twin tracks of the SAK line head off eastwards. At the first survey date these tracks were in position but hardly used. They were kept open for grain trains delivering to a whisky distillery, and perhaps Alloa-bound passengers might raise a glass to that.

The Alloa branch was originally North British Railway.

The traffic lights on the junction to the Tesco store might be a distraction at night.

Stirling North is 118 miles 38 chains (190.7km) from Carlisle.

Dunblane (DB)

Date Built	1900
CR Type or Builder	Caledonian Type N3+
No. of Levers	60
Ways of Working	AB
Current Status	Active
Listed (Cat/N)	N

Dunblane is a delightful town on the Allan Water, and its chief claim to fame nowadays is that it is the home of tennis ace Andy Murray.

The station is a charmingly preserved set of buildings, most of which have found other uses now, which is usually resplendent with flower tubs and the like courtesy of a group called Dunblane in Bloom.

There are three platforms – two for the up and down services from Stirling to Perth, and one for services that terminate at Dunblane from Edinburgh and Glasgow – so it is clearly an important commuter station and local hub.

Fig. 338 shows a CR box with the timber cladding rather than brickwork and a substantial box mindful of the layout now. Dunblane had been the junction for the Callender and Oban line that crossed the West Highland at Crianlarich before both went their separate ways to sea ports. The line from Dunblane to Crianlarich was closed in the 1960s; Oban is still reached via Crianlarich but by former North British metals.

In Fig. 339 the platform 2 starter, DB 45, is centre stage. There is a class 66 past the box waiting for the road behind a home signal. The loop on the left is from platform 3; trains arrive on the down side and go into the platform. The ones that turn back here then go under the bridge, where there is a trailing crossover so the trains can regain platform 1 to go back on the up line.

Fig. 339   Dunblane station, north end and signals, September 2007.

Fig. 338   Dunblane signal box, September 2007.

Fig. 340   Dunblane station looking towards Stirling, September 2007.

Fig. 341   Greenloaning signal box, September 2007.

Fig. 340 gives the opposite view of the station's three platforms, with the DB 45 signal post on the left. The First Scotrail class 156, 156 449, has got the road for the south, and the underslung bracket signal telling us that is right by the leading cab of the DMU. The Strathclyde Partnership for Transport (SPT) class 170 Turbostar would seem to have arrived on a Glasgow service. When all passengers have alighted it then rejoins the down main line past platform 2, goes up to the crossover past the box and joins the up main line and platform 1 for the return journey south. The concrete plinth in the foreground would most likely have been a water tank in steam days, with bags for both platforms 2 and 3.

Dunblane station is 123 miles 19 chains (198.3km) from Carlisle.

Greenloaning (GL)

Date Built	1891
CR Type or Builder	Caledonian Type N2+
No. of Levers	32
Ways of Working	AB
Current Status	Active
Listed (Cat/N)	N

Greenloaning is in Perthshire, situated, like Dunblane, on the Allan Water river, though the countryside here is more dramatic and mountainous.

The small community here is mostly occupied with farming; there was a station here but that closed in 1956.

Fig. 342   Greenloaning co-acting signal, September 2007.

Fig. 341 shows Greenloaning signal box. There are up and down loops described as refuge sidings in front of the box. The bracket signal to admit entry to the up side towards Stirling is down the line a way, together with the down home signal towards Perth.

Fig. 342 shows an unusual signal, the like of which we've only seen once before – at Helsby Junction on the Wirral. The home signal by the bridge has co-acting arms: in other words, one signal wire operates two arms so that one of the arms can be seen whether the train is near or far from the bridge. The old station, which is inhabited, and the end loading dock are to the right. The double disc that has its back to us controls reversing into the up refuge siding or reversing over the crossover, from bottom to top respectively.

Fig. 343   Greenloaning cautionary ground signal, September 2007.

Fig. 344   Blackford signal box, September 2007.

Fig. 343 shows another unusual signal. This is a ground disc that allows a locomotive to pass it at caution, thus obviating the need for much moving of the signals when passing the disc, often during shunting. Note how the pulley is secured to the sleeper extension and the flat bar at the back, which is a detector slide. This interlocks with the point tie bar so that only correct indications of the disc and point can be given. The device in the ballast that resembles a medieval thumbscrew is a point blade clamp. In Scotland red-coloured granite ballast was used to some degree.

Blackford (BK)

Date Built	1933
CR Type or Builder	LMS Type 12
No. of Levers	25
Ways of Working	AB
Current Status	Active
Listed (Cat/N)	N

Blackford made an early name for itself with a brewery that enjoyed royal patronage. Later, when the LMS built the Gleneagles Hotel nearby, associated with the famous golf course, many people from Blackford found employment there. The station at Blackford opened in 1848 and has

since closed, but Gleneagles Hotel station is still open.

In Fig. 344 the LMS continues the Caledonian tradition of a lookout window at the front of the box on the larger structures. The box looks spick and span and immune from the changes that war brought about.

The scenery of Perthshire is a fitting backdrop to the bracket signal in Fig. 345 whose subsidiary arm controls entry into the refuge siding, which is on the up side towards Stirling. Opposite the signal post is a numeric indicator on a small post, saying '41'. This cannot be route mileage as it is still calculated from Carlisle at this point, but it is 41 miles (66km) to Glasgow from Blackford. This must be a Caledonian Railway relic.

Note also the rustic railway fencing, some of which has been made from old sleepers. Some early sleepers were mahogany brought back as ballast in British ships that had exported goods to Burma. Mahogany is now considered a valuable hardwood.

The line to which the bracket signal refers is on the left in Fig. 346, and not only is there a refuge siding but a loading bank for sacks of grain. The refuge siding consists of a locomotive run-round loop and two sidings. Note how a train is signalled out of the refuge siding by one of two ground discs that have their backs to us. The view is towards

Fig. 345   Blackford signal box signals, September 2007.

Stirling, and the crossover allows entry to the up refuge sidings. The down refuge siding on the right is an engineer's facility. The lattice post home signal, complete with finial, has to be this tall as the line drops sharply away.

Blackford signal box is 133 miles 28 chains (214.6km) from Carlisle.

Gleneagles Hotel station is just over 2 miles (3.2km) down the line towards Perth.

Auchterarder (AR)

Date Built	1895
CR Type or Builder	Caledonian Type N2
No. of Levers	16
Ways of Working	AB
Current Status	Active
Listed (Cat/N)	N

The burgh town of Auchterarder is notable for a high street that is 1½ miles (2.5km) long, and for wide drainage streams that had to be bridged before the front door could be reached. Maybe this is a sort of Highland Bourton-on-the-Water.

Golf is big here, as the town has its own course as well as Gleneagles just up the road.

Auchterarder signal box is another splendidly preserved Caledonian example that has had the usual steps, porch and rear admin block added to modernize (Fig. 347). There are just up and down refuge sidings here.

Fig. 346   Blackford refuge and engineer's sidings and signals, September 2007.

Fig. 347   Auchterarder signal box, September 2007.

Fig. 348   Auchterarder lattice post signal, September 2007.

Fig. 348 is another shot of a lattice post signal, without finial this time; these signals will be in the hen's teeth department before long although there are some fine examples of Scottish signalling at the Bo'ness and Kinneil and the Strathspey preserved railways.

Auchterarder signal box is 137 miles and 41 chains (221.3km) from Carlisle.

Hilton Junction (HJ)

Date Built	1895
CR Type or Builder	Caledonian Type N2
No. of Levers	16
Ways of Working	AB
Current Status	Active
Listed (Cat/N)	N

We are now just a couple of miles from Perth, the city immortalized by Sir Walter Scott in his 1828 novel *The Fair Maid of Perth* – the city has been known as the Fair City ever since. It is indeed a beautiful city on the banks of the River Tay, with many fine buildings – among them Scone Abbey, where the kings of Scotland were crowned.

Hilton Junction signal box, in Fig. 349, is not so grand but performs a valuable function. The line we have been travelling on comes in on the right and there is a trailing crossover before the junction. Although this is a double junction, the line on the left, ex-North British towards Edinburgh, becomes single track within half a mile of the junction. Note how the signal wire changes direction to head off under the ballast to the up side of the Scottish Central line of the journey. Just after the junction is the 1,210yd (1,106m) Moncrieffe Tunnel.

Perth was a joint station owned by the Caledonian, North British and Highland Railways. In steam days ex-LNER A4 Pacifics could be seen with ex-LMS Duchess Pacifics. Perth yard had a locomotive turntable until recent years.

Fig. 350 is a side view of Hilton Junction signal box and the outsize admin block on the end. Could it be that wet rooms are now provided?

Hilton Junction signal box is 149 miles 23 chains (240.3km) from Carlisle.

We now return to the Falkirk area to Fouldubs Junction.

Fig. 349   Hilton Junction signal box, September 2007.

Fig. 350   Hilton Junction signal box side view, September 2007.

Fouldubs Junction (FD)

Date Built	1908
CR Type or Builder	Caledonian Type N3
No. of Levers	40
Ways of Working	AB
Current Status	Active
Listed (Cat/N)	N

This is now North British territory, strictly speaking, but where there were joint interests the signalling infrastructure was shared. The box at Grangemouth Junction was originally North British and is now a Portakabin.

Fouldubs Junction had seen passengers as late as 1968 but is now freight only around the Grangemouth docks. There was a plan to update the facilities hereabouts as the sidings were considered not long enough for modern trains. The survey pre-dates those changes.

Fig. 351 is the view from Beancross Road in Grangemouth. Although the box has only nine point rods coming out of it, they seem to be getting their fair share of attention. Note the smaller-armed home signal right by the box; this is to allow exit from the 'branch', which curves away to the right underneath the M9 motorway. The branch is now a container depot.

There are two other tracks coming in from the left to run past the box, and they are the up and down main running lines from Grangemouth Junction. The down goods line into the docks area has a fixed-arm home signal, which is rare; presumably trains brought to a stand here had to be hand signalled past the signal post from the box.

Fig. 352 shows the view from the other side of Beancross Road overbridge. The line on the left is the exit line from the container depot mentioned above. The lines continue around the curve to another container terminal.

The two other lines are the continuation of the up and down freight lines that came from Grangemouth Junction. Now these lines become single up and down lines: the left hand leading to

Fig. 351   Fouldubs Junction signal box, September 2007.

Fig. 352   Fouldubs Junction with docks, container depot and oil terminal lines, September 2007.

Grangemouth Docks, and the right to the oil terminal and an oil and gas terminal.

Although this is a freight-only line, much of it is track circuited and some of it has facing-point locks. We have seen this level of protection before in the nuclear industry and it is obviously policy, when considering potentially dangerous cargo, to employ all safeguards as would be used on passenger-carrying lines. Someone had to do a risk assessment.

Fouldubs Junction signal box is 1 mile 51 chains (2.6km) from Grangemouth Junction.

Perth to Aberdeen

This journey is different in that the line was a joint line but that the companies built their own buildings in certain places but not others. The journey begins in Caledonian Railway territory and then languishes for some time with the North British before reverting back to the CR. That does not affect the glorious mountain and coastal scenery that accompanies most of the route. The schematic diagram in Fig. 353 is not to scale but includes all the NBR signal boxes en route so that we can see them in context; a study of each box will have to wait for the LNER volumes in this series, to which they and the Great North of Scotland Railway belong.

Mileages for the first part of the journey are now calculated from Dundee West.

Barnhill (BH)

Date Built	1874
CR Type or Builder	Caledonian Type N1
No. of Levers	20
Ways of Working	TBR, AB
Current Status	Active
Listed (Cat/N)	N

The line from Perth station is single track for less than a mile over the Tay viaduct then becomes double track for the journey to Dundee. The box works tokenless block regulation, which means that a single line is operated without tokens, and in this case without the tokenless block instruments either, but in accordance with the regulations.

The principles of tokenless block are as follows. Let us suppose that a train is being passed from Perth power box to Barnhill.

1. Both boxes must set their block instruments to Normal to begin a movement.
2. Perth then offers the train to Barnhill with a bell code description of the type of train it is.
3. If Barnhill accepts the train, both block instruments will show Train Accepted.
4. Perth can then pull off the signals for the train

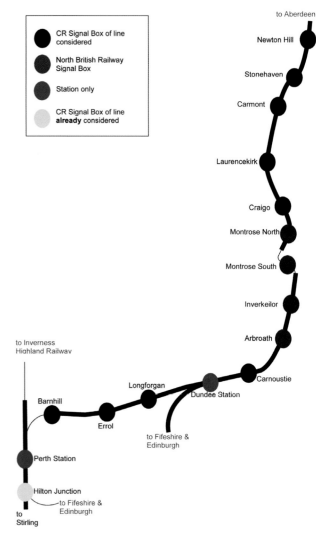

Fig. 353   Caledonian Railway, Perth–Aberdeen schematic diagram.

to proceed. This has the effect of locking any signals at danger that would authorize a move in the opposite direction.

5. Only when the Barnhill signaller has witnessed the tail lamp of the train entering the next section can the block instrument be returned to Normal. Train out of Section is given to Perth, who can then return their instrument to Normal.
6. The system is then ready to start a new move in either direction. No doubt track circuits provide additional safeguards.

There is normally provision for a 'shunt into section' facility from either end using a shunting key, which is interlocked with instruments to prevent a train entering a section while shunting is being carried out.

As there are no tokenless block instruments here, the regulations have been relaxed to allow shunting into the section by setting the home signal to off to enter the section. No train could be sent from the other end anyway, as the action of pulling off at one end locks any pulling off in the opposite direction, and the block instruments are interlocked as well.

The full Scottish tokenless block system, with instruments, will be described in the section about Barrhead at the end of this chapter.

In Fig. 354 the single line starts 160yd (146m) to the right in the Perth direction. The home signal would be to hold a train at the box while another coming from Perth was occupying the single line.

Barnhill signal box is 19 miles and 69 chains (32km) from Dundee West.

Fig. 354   Barnhill signal box, September 2007.

Errol (ER)

Date Built	1877
CR Type or Builder	Caledonian Type N1
No. of Levers	20
Ways of Working	AB
Current Status	Active
Listed (Cat/N)	B

Errol sits on the banks of the River Tay and was famous for its reeds, which were used for making thatched roofs.

The Earl of Erroll (*sic*) was an ancient title but one of its more recent holders was Jocelyn Victor Hay, the 22nd Earl who was the playboy murdered in Kenya in 1941. This scandalized Britain at a time when the nation was enduring hardships and nightly bombing. Cheshire baronet Sir Jock Delves Broughton, whose wife had had a liaison with the earl, stood trial for murder but was acquitted. The case was the subject of book and film *White Mischief*, as well as subsequent TV programmes.

The station was closed in 1985 but was looked after by the Errol Station Trust and so was largely intact at the time of the survey. There are three engineer's sidings there as well but they are described as 'not in regular use' (NIRU). In addition there is a trailing crossover to enable the up running line towards Perth to access the sidings.

Errol signal box is in good condition in Fig. 355, as might be expected for a listed building, although listing is no guarantee of good treatment. The surrounding home semaphore signals contrast with the two distant colour light signals. Note the pile of the red granite ballast in the yard behind the box.

Fig. 356 shows Errol station with a wall plaque (actually 1950s) proclaiming 1847, in BR Scottish

Fig. 355   Errol signal box, September 2007.

Fig. 356   Errol station and footbridge, September 2007.

Fig. 358   Errol lattice post signal, September 2007.

Fig. 357   Errol signals, September 2007.

Region light blue colours. The footbridge looks as though it might be something found at an adventure park, with no timber decking.

The very tall home signals in Fig. 357 are usually an indication that the line drops down either side; the height aids visibility. The view is towards Dundee.

Opposite Errol signal box, Fig. 358 is a detailed view of the lattice post home signal. The ladder appears to be a later galvanized steel replacement. Note that there is still a backlight blinder even though this signal is right opposite the box. That grey box appears to be a motor and sometimes, even though the signal was close to the

box, signals would be motorized because of signal wire routing problems to do with the crossing, or similar reason.

Errol signal box is 10 miles 45 chains (17km) from Dundee West.

Longforgan (LN)

Date Built	1929
CR Type or Builder	LMS Type 12
No. of Levers	20
Ways of Working	AB, TCB
Current Status	Active
Listed (Cat/N)	N

Only a few miles from Dundee, Longforgan is another pretty and ancient village with connections to the aristocracy.

In October 1979 there was a fatal railway accident just down the line. The nearest station is Invergowrie, and that is the place ascribed to the accident, but Longforgan box was involved.

A passenger train headed by a class 25 diesel locomotive was coming from Glasgow Queen Street station and heading for Dundee. The locomotive passed Longforgan box and the signal was returned to danger behind it, once the signaller had ascertained that the fifth coach was carrying the tail lamp. After this, a traction motor on the class 25 caught fire and the train was halted near Invergowrie Bay, which is less than 2 miles (3.2km) from the box.

Then a Glasgow–Aberdeen express, hauled by a class 47 locomotive, was halted at the box home signal, which was subsequently cleared to off. The locomotive then moved slowly along to the starter signal, which was still on, or at danger. Testimony given stated that the signal arm was raised by about 4 degrees, which may have been an adjustment issue, though it was still showing a red light. The locomotive then accelerated into the section, past the home signal at danger and hit the stationary Dundee train at an estimated 60mph (100km/h). There were five deaths and fifty-one injuries.

The subsequent enquiry revealed some deficiencies in the equipment.

Firstly, the signal post had been bent or struck by a passing wagon chain or similar, and this explained the slight 'off' aspect when it should have been danger or on.

Secondly, there was no signal adjuster wire as we have seen at Prestatyn in Chapter 3, although these are usually only fitted on distant signals.

Thirdly, there was no repeater in the box to confirm the signal's aspect; and lastly, there was no AWS, which would have confirmed the starter signal's aspect to the express driver by an audible warning, although again these are more often fitted at distant signal locations.

The report does not mention track circuiting and the assumption is that the track circuit would not have prevented the signaller either from raising the starter signal with a train in the section ahead or from offering it forward to Dundee power box.

Longforgan signal box, in Fig. 359, has only a crossing and block post responsibilities.

The signals may have been moved since the accident, but the signal in Fig. 360 must be the home signal in question. Note the signal wire posts and wires stop at this signal, so any other signals up the line must be colour lights. This signal is track circuited.

With the same proviso about signals moving, the signal in Fig. 361 must be the box starter signal for the next section, towards Invergowrie and Dundee, the city in the distance. Note the colour light signal on the up side towards Perth.

Longforgan signal box is 5 miles 55 chains (9.2km) from Dundee West.

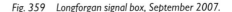

Fig. 359   Longforgan signal box, September 2007.

Fig. 360   Longforgan signal towards Perth, September 2007.

Fig. 361   *Longforgan signal towards Dundee, September 2007.*

Fig. 362   *Carnoustie signal box, September 2007.*

Dundee, on the banks of the silvery Tay, grew in importance with the jute spinning industry used for sacking and hessian. The city expanded still further with the growing of soft fruits and the preserve industry, with Keiller a prominent name. Dundee was also the home of DC Thomson comics, publishers of the *Dandy* and the *Beano*, among others.

This was all summed up in the city's epithet 'jute, jam and journalism' – although into that mix must be put the American Timex watch company, who notoriously closed their factory here in response to a workers' strike in 1993.

Dundee is also home to the Tay Railway Bridge, which blew down for the first time in 1879 after Queen Victoria had travelled over it and its builder was knighted. However, that is a North British Railway story.

Carnoustie (CA)

Date Built	1898
CR Type or Builder	Caledonian Type N2
No. of Levers	20
Ways of Working	TCB, AB
Current Status	Active
Listed (Cat/N)	N

Carnoustie, in the county of Angus, is world famous as a golf course and actually has three. The championship course has hosted the Open seven times up to time of publication and numerous other golf tournaments.

Carnoustie has a regular station and a further halt called Golf Street. The station has refuge sidings on the down side with the remnants of a loading dock.

Fig. 362 shows Carnoustie signal box sharing its location with the North Sea. Carnoustie championship course is, apparently, very challenging, and a good many golf balls end up in the sea or the Barry Burn (stream) that runs through the main course, which is off to the right.

Fig. 363   *Carnoustie signals, crossover and loading dock, September 2007.*

Fig. 363 is the view towards Golf Street Halt and Dundee. The refuge siding and what appears to be a loading dock are on the right. Note how the trap points would tip a vehicle off into the loading dock wall if it were to transgress. There are just ground discs here for signalling company although there is a platform starter on the down side towards Aberdeen across the crossing.

Carnoustie signal box is 10 miles 29 chains (16.7km) from the former Dundee East station.

There follows an extended piece of coastline, including Arbroath and Montrose, which is joint North British Railway territory until we get right on the border of Angus at Craigo.

The loading dock on the down running line towards Aberdeen is a curious feature, as is the beached cabin cruiser (Fig. 365). The refuge siding on the near up side, with ground disc exit signal, trap point and rusty rails, looks out of use. Signallers have said, however, that while all this stuff looks derelict, it has to be maintained and tested regularly just in case a train needs to use it, probably in an emergency. The Grampian Hills and Aberdeen beckon in the distance.

Now that we are back on purely Caledonian metals as distinct from joint with the NBR, the mileages change to be calculated from Carlisle again.

Craigo signal box is 205 miles 15 chains (330.2km) from Carlisle.

Craigo (CO)

Date Built	*c.*1877
CR Type or Builder	Caledonian Type N2
No. of Levers	21
Ways of Working	AB
Current Status	Active
Listed (Cat/N)	N

Craigo is a village some 5 miles (8km) north of Montrose that developed with the aid of textiles. Craigo lost its railway station in 1956. According to Network Rail, Craigo signal box can now be opened or switched out as required.

Fig. 364 shows the signal box and you can see a side-mounted ladder to the lattice post signal although the finial has gone walkabout. Note the pulley at the bottom of the post turning the lever through 90 degrees to activate the signal arm.

Fig. 364   Craigo signal box, September 2007.

Fig. 365   Craigo loading dock and cabin cruiser, September 2007.

Laurencekirk (LK)

Date Built	1910
CR Type or Builder	Caledonian Type N2+
No. of Levers	40
Ways of Working	AB
Current Status	Active
Listed (Cat/N)	N

Laurencekirk is a small town in what is now Aberdeenshire, whose main claim to fame was the manufacture of snuff boxes. Snuff is powdered tobacco and was used in polite society when the only other method of taking tobacco was by clay pipe. Later on it became the preserve of those occupations where smoking is forbidden, for example coal mining.

Left to its own devices, tobacco dries out, making it unusable, so the manufacturers introduced an airtight lid to their snuff boxes, called the Laurencekirk lid.

Laurencekirk had a station until 1968 and it was reopened in 2009 after the survey. However, the wooden goods shed was still in being and the yard was busy, which was remarkable.

Laurencekirk has the up refuge siding in front of the box and the down goods loop and goods yard on the side opposite to the box (Fig. 366). The signal box is another well-preserved if modernized structure but a relative youngster, dating from the Edwardian period.

All four sidings in Fig. 367 are occupied by the train of pipes, which are being unloaded by a road crane. The triple ground discs all in a row is a first. The pipes are unlikely to be for natural gas but Britain is criss-crossed by pipelines for either fuel or chemicals. While they are expensive to put in, they reduce road traffic, which is good; but they have also affected rail traffic, as much of this used to go by 100-tonne rail tankers. Rail accidents in the United States and Canada go a long way to argue that pipelines are safer, however – the Quebec oil train derailment in 2013 claimed forty-seven lives. This pipeline project is a long one, as photographs show pipes being unloaded twelve months before the survey date.

Fig. 367   Laurencekirk goods yard, September 2007.

Fig. 366   Laurencekirk signal box, September 2007.

Fig. 368   Laurencekirk goods shed, September 2007.

The wooden goods shed in Fig. 368 looks a bit the worse for wear but recognizable and still containing track within for the loading and unloading of wagons. There would usually be a hand crane within these structures but there isn't one here, which could point to sacks of grain as likely merchandise in steam days. Locomotives were not usually permitted inside goods sheds and wagons would often be moved in and out of the shed using a pinch bar, which is a big lever. The mark one shoulder also came into play, while very busy yards might have a steam-driven capstan. Shunting horses were in use until the early 1960s. The problem was not getting the wagon to move, but stopping it where it was needed.

Note the original station buildings on the right. There is a portable floodlight on the left so the pipeline operation must be of some urgency.

Although the platform has gone, the station in Fig. 369 looks as though it could function as such again. Note how the brick-built station has been cement rendered to keep out the winter winds and rain. The signal box and signals are in the background and the view is towards Aberdeen.

Laurencekirk signal box is 210 miles 62 chains (339.2km) from Carlisle.

Carmont (CM)

Date Built	1876
CR Type or Builder	Caledonian Type N1+
No. of Levers	18
Ways of Working	AB
Current Status	Active
Listed (Cat/N)	N

To describe Carmont as a hamlet is to exaggerate. There are just a few buildings at the crossing of road and rail.

The railway has been a few miles from the North Sea but now turns inland before keeping the sea company to Aberdeen.

Fig. 369   Laurencekirk old station, box and signals, September 2007.

Fig. 370   Carmont signal box, September 2007.

Carmont signal box, in Fig. 370, is mainly concerned with survival in a harsh winter environment. The cement render and stout double-glazed windows must be a comfort when a gale from the North Sea blows in.

In Fig. 371 the line curves inland towards Aberdeen. The home signal expects a train to the Granite City.

Fig. 371   Carmont signals towards Aberdeen, September 2007.

Fig. 372 Carmont and First Scotrail class 170 in turbo mode heading towards Aberdeen, September 2007.

Fig. 373 Stonehaven signal box, September 2007.

In Fig. 372 a First Scotrail class 170 Turbostar from Edinburgh Haymarket depot leans into the curve on its way to Aberdeen. Note the chimney stack on the rear of the box.

Carmont signal box is 219 miles and 39 chains (353.2km) from Carlisle.

Stonehaven (SV)

Date Built	1901
CR Type or Builder	Caledonian Type N2
No. of Levers	40
Ways of Working	AB
Current Status	Active
Listed (Cat/N)	B

Stonehaven was a port from Iron Age times and developed into a centre for the herring fishing trade. With the inception of North Sea oil and development of Aberdeen as its land base, Stonehaven has become a desirable commuter town.

Fig. 373 shows the unusual platform-mounted signal box, which is listed along with the station buildings. Just when you hadn't seen a wooden goods shed for years, two come along. The smaller one behind the box was in use as a garage at the survey date.

The listed station building in Fig. 374 is a splendid edifice, reflecting Stonehaven's importance as a fishing port when it was built. There are planter tubs and a wooden weather barrier further up the platform.

Fig. 375 is the end of platform 2 looking towards Aberdeen and the refuge and shunting sidings on the up side. The platform starter is SV 17, and the other lattice post signal on the up side is to protect the running line when the siding point is changed. Note the loading bank on the up side; it's not

Fig. 374 Stonehaven station, September 2007.

Fig. 375 (left)   Stonehaven signals, refuge siding and crossover, September 2007.

Fig. 376 (above)   Stonehaven signals towards Carlisle and Dundee, September 2007.

difficult to imagine boxes of herring being loaded into covered wagons after the boxes had been stuffed with ice for the onward journey to Glasgow, London and elsewhere in Britain. Note the red granite ballast in use here.

Fig. 376 is the opposite view to Fig. 375 and shows the line back to Carmont and Carlisle. The HST is allowed 85mph (137km/h) on the curve whilst a DMU can only do 75mph (120km/h). The crossover is to allow access to the down refuge siding so there are two crossovers here, as the refuge sidings are at opposite ends of the station.

Stonehaven station is 224 miles 74 chains (362km) from Carlisle.

Newtonhill (NH)

Date Built	*c*.1876
LCR Type or Builder	Caledonian Type N1+
No. of Levers	30
Ways of Working	AB, TCB
Current Status	Active
Listed (Cat/N)	N

About 10 miles (16km) from Aberdeen, Newtonhill was originally called Skateraw, and developed as a fishing village with the addition of smoke houses to produce kippers or smoked herring. The village had a station called Skateraw, but that closed in 1956.

Newtonhill signal box, in Fig. 377, has the plain, large-paned windows of Laurencekirk rather than the attempt at listing compliance of Stonehaven. There are five point rods coming out of the box, and they are for refuge sidings on each running line and a trailing crossover.

In Fig. 378 the bracket signal gives a better view from curved track. The building behind the signal is a lamp room by the look of it, with hazard warnings on the door. Oddly, though, the building had a chimney at one time.

Fig. 377   Newtonhill signal box, September 2007.

Fig. 378   Newtonhill bracket signal and lamp hut, September 2007.

Fig. 379   Newtonhill calling on signal in lattice post configuration, September 2007.

Fig. 380   Barrhead signal box, October 2014.

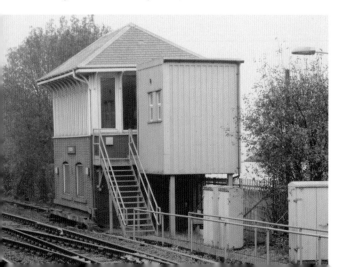

Fig. 379 shows a real curiosity of a signal that admits entry to a siding. The construction is such that the signal is giving out the message that, even when off, the siding must be approached with the utmost caution. Oddities such as these quite often relate to some event in the distant past.

Newtonhill signal box is 230 miles 59 chains (371.3km) from Carlisle.

Aberdeen is known as the 'Granite City' and has many fine mainly Victorian buildings. The quarried granite has a high mica content and the buildings are said to sparkle in sunlight.

A centre for the northeast coast fishing industry, the harbour is now almost exclusively devoted to the offshore oil industry, and there is a helicopter base nearby at Dyce to service the rigs in the North Sea.

Glasgow

The final Caledonian Railway signal box is at Barrhead south of Glasgow. It is the sole survivor of an intense suburban network around the city that has been almost completely modernized. In Volume 1, the Glasgow and South Western Railway journey from Annan near Carlisle brought us up to Kilmarnock and Lugton signal box, which was the extent of that line's operation.

Barrhead (BD)

Date Built	1894
CR Type or Builder	Caledonian Type S4
No. of Levers	25
Ways of Working	TCB, AB
Current Status	Active
Listed (Cat/N)	N

In and around Glasgow was considered to be the south division of the Caledonian Railway and so all signal boxes have the 'S' prefix to the type number. So far all CR boxes were considered to be north division and are so prefixed. The south division, exemplified in Fig. 380, would seem to be more ornate.

Fig. 381 Barrhead signal box and bay platform looking towards Glasgow, October 2014.

Fig. 382 All change! Barrhead station and bay platform looking towards Kilmarnock, October 2014.

Fig. 381 shows the north end of Barrhead station looking towards Glasgow, which becomes a terminus for Glasgow Central station suburban services. The bay platform is for a dedicated Glasgow service and the two other platforms would appear to be used for that as well, as the far platform is bi-directionally signalled. The far platform is also for departing trains for Kilmarnock in the opposite direction, where the line becomes single track. Note the trap point from the bay and the modernized colour light signal, compared with the main line versions. Note also the crossover by the box to bring trains departing towards Glasgow from the far platform 1 onto the correct running line. Not surprisingly, this crossover has facing-point locks.

Fig. 382 is looking towards Kilmarnock. Platform 1, on the far left, sees class 156 loco, 156 509, has the road, with the green colour light signal in the distance, for Kilmarnock. Class 156, 156 446, has the caption 'Central' and will depart towards the camera from platform 2. On the far right, class 156, 156 506, also waits to depart on a Glasgow service from platform 3.

Scottish Tokenless Block System

The principle of operation is the same as we have seen in England in that it is a way of speeding up operation on single lines by removing the need for trains to stop to exchange tokens. It involves special block instruments that interlock to ensure that conflicting moves cannot be set up on single lines.

The special block instruments are peculiar to Scotland and were manufactured there. There are several variants of equipment – that shown in Fig. 383 is in use on the Carlisle–Glasgow ex-GSWR

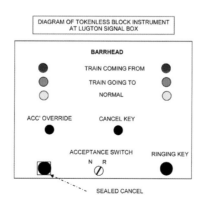

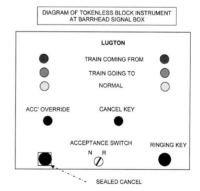

Fig. 383 Scottish tokenless block instrument, schematic diagram.

main line. A different type is shown under Kilkerran signal box in Volume 1 of this book.

Fig. 383 is a simplified, not-to-scale diagram of the Scottish tokenless block equipment. The following section describes how trains are passed from box to box under the Scottish route tokenless block regulations and what impact it might have on other equipment.

Before the passage of a train can begin, both signallers must ensure that the shunting key, which permits a train to shunt within a TB section, is withdrawn from the frame. In addition, any previous train must have sent or received Train out of Section from both boxes.

The Normal white light on the diagram is the state of the section at the beginning and end of a move and it is taken to mean Line Blocked. This may not actually be the case, but this is to indicate that positive confirmation is required from the signaller that the line is clear each time.

For the sake of the example we will assume that the train leaving platform 1 at Barrhead in Fig. 382 for Lugton and Kilmarnock is the one being passed to Lugton signal box.

In the table below the text in **bold** indicates a signal box that has instigated an action.

It is not actually quite as simple as this as the signallers must operate points and signals to coincide with the move being undertaken. Also note that there is provision to cancel a move or override an acceptance. Lugton then repeats this process to pass the train to Kilmarnock.

From Barrhead	To Lugton	Note
Call attention RK	Ack call attention RK	
Line clear? RK (bell code)	Ack line clear RK (bell code)	Lugton select R for reverse on AS
RK hold 5 secs	Train coming from (indication)	Opposite direction signals locked
	RK hold 5 secs	
Train going to (indication)		Barrhead can clear signals
Train entering section	Ack train entering section	
	Call attention RK	When Lugton sees tail lamp
Ack call attention	**Set AS to normal**	
	Train out of section RK	
Ack TOS RK 5 secs		Restores the locking to normal

RK = ringing key
AS = acceptance switch

CHAPTER 4

Highland Railway (HR)

The Highland Railway, in 1923, contributed some 494 route miles (795km) to the LMS total. The main line from Perth to Inverness is mostly single track, worked under Scottish tokenless block regulations and tackling the highest point of any main line in Britain in the Grampian Mountains. At Inverness the main line carries on to Wick and Thurso, and this was a destination for the Welsh steam coal trains covered in the GWR book in this series during World War I.

Some of the coal trains were sent to Grangemouth and then the coal was shipped north from there.

The consumer was the Grand Fleet at Scapa Flow and the garrison of 4,000 at Invergordon. The Highland Railway saw freight traffic volumes many times the pre-war norm.

To the west there is an iconic branch line to Kyle of Lochalsh, which is a ferry terminal for the Western Isles and a beautifully scenic line to boot.

To the east the line heads off along the northeast coast towards Aberdeen but becomes the Great North of Scotland Railway (GNoSR), and therefore LNER territory after Elgin.

As there has not been much change, other than the usual branch line culling, much of the line is as it was, and retains many steam age features.

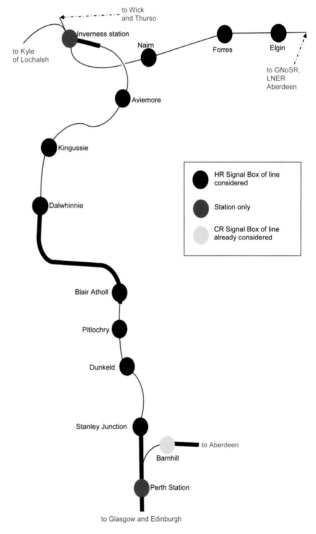

Fig. 384   Highland Railway schematic diagram.

Fig. 385   Stanley Junction signal box, September 2007.

Fig. 386   Stanley Junction home signals, September 2007.

The simplified, not-to-scale schematic diagram in Fig. 384 shows the journey to be taken, starting at Stanley Junction near Perth.

Stanley Junction (SJ)

Date Built	1961
HR Type or Builder	BR Scottish Region Non-Standard
No. of Levers	45
Ways of Working	AB, TB
Current Status	Active
Listed (Cat/N)	N

Stanley Junction had a station and other sidings before 1956, when the station was closed. It was a junction with the CR line to Forfar and the east coast, since closed.

It is now a single point or turnout, where the double track from Perth goes into one and the line becomes TB worked from there to Dunkeld and beyond. The box was built after the station closed so seems rather large in view of its duties and scope in Fig. 385. The view is towards Dunkeld.

The double track from Perth must be bi-directionally signalled, as the two semaphore home signals in Fig. 386 relate to the double lines from Perth.

Stanley Junction signal box is 7 miles 8 chains (11.4km) from Perth.

Dunkeld (DK)

Date Built	1919
HR Type or Builder	Highland
No. of Levers	23
Ways of Working	TB
Current Status	Active
Listed (Cat/N)	N

Dunkeld is a cathedral town of some antiquity, and it is said that musket ball pock marks from a battle in 1689 are still visible on the cathedral today. The town follows more peaceful pursuits now and is popular with walkers and tourists. It stands on the banks of the River Tay, and the salmon in the river promoted the growth of smoke houses to process

Fig. 387   Dunkeld signal box, September 2007.

Fig. 388   Dunkeld starter signal and loop signals, September 2007.

Fig. 389   Dunkeld station and footbridge, September 2007.

the fish. The quality of Dunkeld smoked salmon is renowned.

In Fig. 387 Dunkeld signal box even has flower tubs on the token apparatus stand, which is not surprising as tokens are not in use here any longer. Tokenless block was invented in the 1960s. Note the bullhead-railed track on the loop line in front of the box.

Fig. 388 shows the up, Perth-bound platform at Dunkeld and Birnham station. The engineer's siding on the left has its own ground disc, and opposite the ground disc a single-railed trap point. They are not as common as the double-railed type. The graceful lattice post signal with finial contrasts with the rather more workaday bracket signal that allows access to either station platform. The single line recommences right after the bracket signal.

Fig. 389 shows Dunkeld and Birnham station looking towards Pitlochry. The platforms were built in the days when railway coaches had multiple steps to enable access to lower structures. Network

Rail has provided wooden steps that need to be lined up with coach doors. In the 1960s, porter's barrows made admirable mobile seats.

Note the two posts on the opposite ends of the footbridge. They would be places where oil lamps would be parked at night, and possibly later on Tilley lamps, which are pressurized paraffin lamps, before electricity got to the station. The solid stone Victorian station building is reminiscent of the Midland Railway style and worth. The box is just to the left of the footbridge.

Dunkeld signal box is 15 miles 25 chains (24.6km) from Perth.

Pitlochry (PT)

Date Built	1911
HR Type or Builder	Highland +
No. of Levers	24
Ways of Working	TB
Current Status	Active
Listed (Cat/N)	A

Still in Perth and Kinross, Pitlochry developed largely in Victorian times and was given the royal seal of approval by Queen Victoria, who was a visitor before Balmoral was purchased in 1852. She arrived in 1842 and the railway in 1863. The town is very popular with walkers and coach tourists. There is a salmon ladder to aid the fish's progress past the power station up the River Tummel during the breeding season.

Fig. 390   Pitlochry signal box, September 2007.

Fig. 391   Pitlochry station looking towards Perth, September 2007.

Fig. 390 shows the A listed Pitlochry signal box, based on a McKenzie and Holland of Worcester design. Note the massive admin block on the end, about half the size of the box.

Fig. 392   Pitlochry station looking towards Inverness, September 2007.

Fig. 391 gives a glimpse of the station, which is also A listed. The line back to Perth is already running through delightful scenery. Note that the inbound home signal admits a train to the loop on one side only, and that the disabled-friendly platform ends have been raised to facilitate wheelchair access to trains.

Fig. 392 is the view to the north towards Blair Atholl, and an elegant lattice post signal guards the way. The engineer's siding is complete with double-railed trap point and ground disc this time. There's no sign of any goods sheds, so presumably they were timber and have not survived. The loop line is much longer than the platforms, and perhaps this is to enable a freight train or HST to pass another train here.

Pitlochry signal box is 28 miles 31 chains (45.7km) from Perth

Blair Atholl (BA)

Date Built	1891
HR Type or Builder	McKenzie and Holland Type 3
No. of Levers	17 and IFS panel
Ways of Working	TB, AB
Current Status	Active
Listed (Cat/N)	N

Blair Atholl is one of the few pieces of flat ground in the Grampian Mountain region. Blair Castle is the home of the Duke of Atholl, who has a unique royal dispensation to raise a private army. The militia is known as the Atholl Highlanders and is now retained for ceremonial and tourism duties. Blair Atholl has a thriving tourism scene and a whisky distillery.

From here the railway climbs on double track to the Drumuachdar Pass, which, at 1,484ft (452m), is the highest point on the standard gauge network in Britain. With absolute block working if a train is occupying a section, no other train can be admitted. With freight trains taking up to four times as long as the fastest passenger train, this could lead to delays whilst a section was vacated. The intermediate block section, or IBS, splits long block sections up and is in addition to the existing section. In this case there are two IBSs so it is like having three sections instead of one. The IBSs tend to rely on colour light signals that are easily automatically controlled. The movement of a train out of an IBS will clear that section for the signaller and reset signals accordingly. Once a train has passed into an IBS, a further train can be accepted into the original block section.

Fig. 393 shows Blair Atholl signal box at the Perth single line end of the station.

The lattice post home signal in Fig. 394 is for trains to Perth, bracketed out possibly because of the footbridge down the platform.

Fig. 395 shows Blair Atholl station looking towards the double-track section to Dalwhinnie. The oil lamp poles on the footbridge have been converted to accept electric lamps. The station building is on a less imposing scale than we have seen so far but the wooden platform shelter on the down side compensates for that. The building with the wet roof on the left in the distance looks like a stone-built goods shed that is in the down sidings. These sidings are so far from the box that they have their own ground frame.

Fig. 393 Blair Atholl signal box, September 2007.

Fig. 395 Blair Atholl station platforms and buildings, September 2007.

Fig. 394 Blair Atholl signal box and starter signal, September 2007.

Fig. 396 Dalwhinnie signal box, September 2007.

Dalwhinnie (DW)

Date Built	*c.*1909
HR Type or Builder	Highland+
No. of Levers	20 and IFS panel
Ways of Working	TB, AB
Current Status	Active
Listed (Cat/N)	N

Dalwhinnie sits at about 1,170ft (357m) and is one of the coldest villages in Britain, and revels in a multitude of outdoor activities, including hill walking and mountaineering. As a compensation there is a large whisky distillery that produces a single malt whisky of the name Dalwhinnie.

Dalwhinnie signal box has clearly had the builders in, as an extension is all too apparent in Fig. 396. It's a pity they didn't put a third locking room window in while they were at it.

Fig. 397 looks north towards Inverness and a train is signalled from the north. Note the steam age water tower base on the down platform. This time the up platform, which the camera is on, is bi-directionally signalled and the engineer's siding entry point has a facing-point lock on it too. Note how the platforms have been ramped up from their previous low-altitude setting. There aren't too many trees here so the ones at this end of the station

Fig. 397 Dalwhinnie station and signal box looking towards Inverness, September 2007.

Fig. 398 Dalwhinnie signals towards Perth, September 2007.

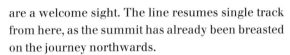

Fig. 399 (left)   Kingussie signal box, September 2007.

Fig. 400 (above)   Kingussie station and signal box, September 2007.

are a welcome sight. The line resumes single track from here, as the summit has already been breasted on the journey northwards.

The small bracket signal in Fig. 398 also signals the way for the expected train in Fig. 397. The bracket signal dolls, or posts, indicate that the speed through the far down platform side will be the greater. Note the yellow marker post proclaiming that we are 58½ miles (94.1km) from Perth at that precise point. The platforms only accommodate four-coach trains so any HST will overlap at the ends unless the signal is off; then it could pass the signal post to pull up.

Dalwhinnie signal box is 58 miles 53 chains (94.4km) from Perth.

Kingussie (KG)

Date Built	1894
HR Type or Builder	McKenzie and Holland Type 3, Highland
No. of Levers	17
Ways of Working	TB
Current Status	Active
Listed (Cat/N)	B

Fig. 401   Kingussie station trackwork and signals, September 2007.

Kingussie is remarkable in that it is a world leader in the game of shinty, whose equipment resembles hockey; the game permits mixed-gender teams.

The town is also a noted tourist resort and the beauty of its environs is known to millions as the TV series *Monarch of the Glen* was filmed nearby.

The station is on a larger scale than the other Highland Railway structures and the platforms can accommodate longer trains. Both the signal box and station are grade B listed, which means they are of regional importance.

Kingussie signal box (Fig. 399) is a curious choice for listing in that modernization renders it almost unrecognizable from its original condition. However it is of joint parentage, so perhaps that qualifies it. Note that the station name is repeated in the Gaelic language.

Fig. 400 is a somewhat soggy shot of the platforms and footbridge looking towards Aviemore and Inverness. The small bracket signal doesn't

Fig. 402 Kingussie station and Royal Scotsman luxury train with a class 47 at its head, September 2007.

Fig. 403 Kingussie station and the Royal Scotsman luxury train waits for the arrival of a First Scotrail class 170 DMU, September 2007.

quite do the job apparently, as there is a banner repeater signal at the other end of the platform.

Fig 401 shows the banner repeater referred to in Fig. 400 on the right. The line goes back to single track for the journey to Dalwhinnie. The platforms appear to be bi-directionally signalled only in the up direction heading south. The engineer's siding is on the left.

Fig. 402 shows the Royal Scotsman luxury train in platform 2. The locomotive is likely to be a class 47, 47 804, looking at the West Coast Railways website and the survey date. West Coast supply locomotives for all manner of charter and special trains. They are based at Carnforth, with their depot in the old steam shed and yard there, and were mentioned in Volume 1 in the section on the Furness Railway.

This particular journey of the Royal Scotsman takes three days and two nights, starts at Edinburgh, goes on to Perth, Inverness and Aberdeen and back via the CR/NBR to Dundee and Edinburgh. The current tariff on this all-inclusive trip is about £1,200 or $1,850 per night. Even luxury trains may have to wait on single lines, however, although Kingussie is one of the regular stops for sightseeing.

In Fig. 403 the reason for the line occupation has arrived: a First Scotrail class 170 comes into platform 1.

Kingussie signal box is 71 miles 48 chains (115.2km) from Perth.

Aviemore (AV)

Date Built	1892
HR Type or Builder	McKenzie and Holland Type 3, Highland
No. of Levers	30
Ways of Working	TB, TCB
Current Status	Active
Listed (Cat/N)	B

Aviemore is one of the few places in Britain where snow and skiing can take place with some degree of certainty every year. Consequently it has developed into Britain's premier, perhaps only, ski resort. The town is also popular with walkers in the Cairngorm Mountains.

Aviemore had been a junction of some significance, with an HR branch to Forres on the northeast coast, and a further junction at Boat of Garten on the GNoSR to Elgin and Keith Junction.

Fig. 404 Aviemore signal box, September 2007.

One end of the Strathspey preserved railway, whose other locations are Boat of Garten and Broomhill, is part of the former HR branch. The line runs through beautiful highland scenery, and Boat of Garten is well known as the Osprey village. The eventual destination is Grantown-on-Spey. The Strathspey railway inherited much of the mechanical signalling from Larbert and Carmuirs and it was on display during a simultaneous visit from Aviemore.

Aviemore signal box, in Fig. 404, has reduced in size lever-wise to only thirty levers, but it has a panel to control remote interlocking of stations further north at Carrbridge, Kincraig, Moy, Slochd and Tomatin. Many of these locations previously had signal boxes themselves and Carrbridge's still remains, though not in use by Network Rail. The Strathspey Railway has its own ground frame at Aviemore station, as well as a signal box.

Fig. 405 shows a lattice post bracket whose subsidiary arm controls entry to the engineer's siding up by the box on the far right. There is a further lattice post in front of the bracket, which is a steadying post. Note the two small brackets hanging down underneath the AV 28 plate. They used to hold in place a steel shield that would protect the signal from the blast from a chimney of a steam locomotive. Note the yellow marker post informing us that we are 83½ miles (134.4km) from Perth.

Fig. 406 shows the way to Inverness past the box, engineer's siding and Strathspey Railway. Note the ground frame at the survey date; at the time of the visit they were installing a signal box.

Impressive Aviemore station (Fig. 407) is not listed yet but is surely a candidate. Originally the Strathspey Railway platform on the left was a loop line, so that trains could run in from the south and take the branch to Boat of Garten and beyond if required.

Aviemore station is 83 miles 32 chains (134.2km) from Perth.

Fig. 405 Aviemore lattice post signal and trackwork, September 2007.

Fig. 406 Aviemore plays host to Network Rail and Strathspey Railway tracks, September 2007.

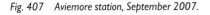

Fig. 407 Aviemore station, September 2007.

Fig. 408   Nairn East signal box, September 2007.

The journey continues to Inverness and then branches out to the northeast coast towards Aberdeen. There is one signal box that was not included in the survey – at Clachnaharry, north of Inverness – and this is a small three-lever box that controls a swing bridge over the Caledonian Canal. Both box and bridge are listed.

Fig. 409   Nairn station building, which is effectively the signal box, September 2007.

Fig. 410   Nairn West signal box, September 2007.

Inverness is the most northern city in Britain and is a fast-growing and economically important hub for the Highlands as well as being an administrative centre for the region.

Nairn (NA)

Date Built	1891
HR Type or Builder	Highland
No. of Levers	Westcad VDUs
Ways of Working	TCB, KT
Current Status	Active
Listed (Cat/N)	B

Nairn is a market town on the northeast coast that has developed into a seaside resort with award-winning beaches. It is also well known for golf, with two championship-standard courses. Its remoteness appeals to those who want to get away from it all, and the town remains unspoilt.

The signal boxes and station building are all listed. The block instruments that were originally installed in the station building have been replaced by computerized displays, still in the station building, which is the actual block post or signal box. The two signal boxes at Nairn West and Nairn East were simply to operate point and signals in the days when this was mechanically done. The signaller was issued with a bicycle to go from one signal box to the other to minimize delays to trains. Both signal boxes are now closed but remain thanks to the listing. The 'box' works key token to Forres as well as TCB to Inverness. Fig. 408 shows Nairn East signal box. The red signal NA 6 has a sign advising that token working applies from here to Forres.

Fig. 409 shows the sturdy and stylish listed station building at Nairn, which actually contains the signalling equipment.

Fig. 410 shows Nairn West, on the way to Inverness. It used to be quite commonplace for block instruments to be housed in the station building and for there to be a separate building for the levers.

This layout was highly criticized as contributing to the Abermule disaster in 1921, and so the trend thereafter was to centralize the instrumentation as well as the levers in one place. The only other place where this situation still obtains is Barrhill, on the Glasgow and South Western Railway route from Ayr to Stranraer, covered in Volume 1.

Nairn station is 128 miles 72 chains (207.4km) from Perth.

Forres (FS)

Date Built	1891
HR Type or Builder	McKenzie and Holland Type 3, Highland
No. of Levers	24
Ways of Working	KT
Current Status	Active
Listed (Cat/N)	N

Forres has been the winner of the Scotland in Bloom award several times and has two whisky distilleries, one of which is preserved by Historic Scotland as a working museum. The town had close associations with RAF Kinloss, which was Britain's main base for the Nimrod aircraft and is now an army barracks.

Forres was a junction station with four platforms at one time, now reduced to one. The line used to run along what is now the Strathspey Railway through Boat of Garten, Grantown-on-Spey and Dava to Forres.

The two key token exchange stages are in view in Fig. 411. For a description of KT working, *see* the section on Bransty signal box, the first box covered in this volume, in Chapter 2. The far semaphore signal is to control the exit from a siding that comes off the run-round loop.

The sole remaining platform at Forres is depicted in Fig. 412 together with the end of the loop just referred to; the box in the distance is looking towards Elgin and Aberdeen. The arrangement of the signals here makes it clear that the loops are uni-directional – a train leaving the platform for Elgin must take the left-hand loop.

Fig. 411   Forres signal box, September 2007.

Fig. 412   Forres station platform and signals, September 2007.

Fig. 413   Rear of Forres signal box, September 2007.

Fig. 414   *Elgin signal box, September 2007.*

Fig. 413 offers a final look at the rear of Forres signal box. McKenzie and Holland of Worcester were notable for their prominent finials.

Forres station is 119 miles 26 chains (192km) from Perth via Dava.

Elgin (EL)

Date Built	1951
HR Type or Builder	Highland
No. of Levers	26
Ways of Working	KT
Current Status	Active
Listed (Cat/N)	N

Fig. 415   *Elgin looking towards Inverness, September 2007.*

Elgin has origins in medieval times and Shakespearian literature with *Macbeth*. The medieval town was swept away in the nineteenth century but the cathedral remains and formed the basis for Elgin's claim to city status. The town was well served by railways, with the Highland Railway coming in from Inverness and the Great North of Scotland Railway from Lossiemouth, Buckie and Craigellachie. This arrival transformed Elgin's fortunes, and the town exported seed potatoes to England by rail as late as 2008.

The box in Fig. 414 has had a chequered history, with the top of the box dating from 1902 and originally being at Mosstowie. Elgin West – so described on the name plate – is the most northerly manually operated signal box in Britain. As well as the key

Fig. 416   *Elgin station and signals looking towards Keith Junction and Aberdeen, September 2007.*

token exchanging platforms, the loop for the station can be seen in the distance.

Fig. 415 shows the view the other way, towards Forres and Inverness. There is a 4-mile (6.5km) branch line leading off the main line to a whisky distiller's and Burghhead but the line hasn't seen a train since 1998, although the tracks remain.

Fig. 416 shows the view from Elgin station platform towards Keith and Aberdeen. Note the subsidiary arm off the bracket for the extensive goods sidings.

Fig. 417 is looking the other way, towards Forres and Inverness, and the box can just be seen by the crossing barriers in the distance.

Remote platform starting signals are a Scottish innovation where a platform starter signal is automatically selected off, along with a section signal.

The sign on the lamppost about remote platform starting signals is the telephone number on the GSM-R network by which the driver can contact the signaller if the signal has failed to go off while the train is at the platform.

Elgin station is 12 miles 18 chains (19.7km) from Forres, where the mileage changes.

Fig. 417 Elgin station and signals looking towards Inverness, with the box in the distance, September 2007.

Useful Resources

Books and Written Works

Allan, I., *British Railways Pre-Grouping Atlas and Gazetteer*

Quail Track Diagrams, Parts 1 and 4 (TrackMaps)

Rolt, L.T.C., *Red for Danger* (Pan Books)

Signalling Record Society, *Signalling Atlas and Signal Box Directory*

The Railway magazine – various issue dates

The works of Adrian Vaughan – various publishers

Websites

Adrian the Rock's signalling pages – www.roscalen.com/signals

Alan Roberts' signalling website – www.6g.nwrail.org.uk/signallingoverwales.htm

The Signalbox by John Hinson – www.signalbox.org

The 8D Association – www.8dassociation.btck.co.uk/signalboxes

IngyTheWingy – www.flickr.com/people/ingythewingy

Wikipedia

Index